# JUST THE EDGE OF GOD

# JUST THE EDGE OF GOD

*The Touch of His Garment is All We Know*

## Ardith Arnelle` Price

Book, Cover Design, and photograph: © Ardith Arnelle` Price

Printed by CreateSpace, An Amazon.com Company

First Edition: May 2015
Printed in the United States of America

ISBN-10:1512093912
ISBN-13:9781512093919

*To my wonderful husband who has applauded my efforts to write an inspirational book and to my deceased parents who inspired me to go as far as the stars and beyond with my talents and gifts from God.*

## TABLE OF CONTENTS

# Preface

Writing this book has been a spiritual journey for me. I was given a commission by God, to write this book two years before I actually started writing. A year ago, I finally settled down enough in my Spirit so I could hear God the Holy Spirit speaks clearly to me. Then God the Holy Spirit started to give me the words to write and once that happened, words just started pouring out of me. The Holy Spirit has empowered me to speak through this book to the End-Time believer.

Who is Jesus? Many people have no idea that Jesus is the Son of God. God has declared that time is short before He returns and we as Christians must get the Word out and save many from damnation. Why did Jesus come to save us? This is what this book is all about. It is about hope, love, and peace of God and therefore explaining who God is to the best of my ability that the Holy Spirit has revealed to me, so that many will be saved before Jesus returns.

For the naysayers this book is not for you. It is for the ones who are sitting on the fence and want to receive peace in their soul. It is for people who have come to the realization of who Jesus is in their lives but have not endorsed the full meaning of Jesus Christ. This inspirational book is for the poor in spirit and the ones seeking to know a higher power, but has failed to realize that Jesus Christ is the only one that can save them and give them peace and love in their souls. For Jesus The Messiah has come and He left a message for the Jewish people to come to Him but they missed the mark at the time of His coming. However, many Jewish people all over the world are coming to know Yeshua (Jesus) and they are fulfilling the prophecy that the Messiah has come and will be here again for the Final

Judgement.  For the Jewish people and the nations of God still have a hard heart toward Jesus the Messiah.  It is time for them to get ready to receive Him now before He returns.  This message is for my Jewish brothers and Sisters, Messianic Jews (those who now know about Jesus), and Christians.

I pray this book will bring comfort, peace, and love to those who read it and come to know Jesus Christ before the tribulation.  The chapters of Zechariah 12 – 14 are critical books to be read with "open eyes and heart" for Jews and Christians throughout the world.  I recommend reading these chapters for further study.  Time waits for no one and the urgency to get ready for Jesus Christ return is paramount because no one knows the day or the hour when Christ will return.

### Ardith Arnelle` Price
Saint of God Almighty, Yeshua HaMashiach (Jesus, the Messiah)

### Note to Readers:
Many Hebrew terms are used though-out the book.  These words identify the person of God for the Gentile reader.  The rational for the Hebraic words is to let the Gentile person know they have a Jewish Father in Heaven.  Christians must be equipped to embrace Hebraic roots in order to understand End-Time prophecy.

# CHAPTER 1

## Just the Edge of God: The Touch of His Garment is All We Know

*In Job 26:14, (NKJV) "Indeed these are the mere edges of HIS ways, and how small a whisper we hear of HIM! But the thunder of HIS power who can understand? He shall judge the world with righteousness and the peoples with HIS truth."*

In Job 26:14, NKJV "Indeed these are the mere edges of HIS ways, and how small a whisper we hear of HIM! But the thunder of HIS power who can understand? He shall judge the world with righteousness and the peoples with HIS truth."

We have heard so many times as Christians that Jesus will be with us no matter what we do in our lives. All we have to do is invoke a prayer and everything will be all right. This is very true however, there is more to that statement and you have to realize that the Word of God is a living breathing Word and you must be careful what you ask for and say with your mouth. "God cannot be mocked" as scripture states (Gal 6:7, AMP). God's words can bring healing and curses depending on the individual case. If you believe with your whole heart, body, mind, and spirit then you will receive the blessing of Jesus Christ the Son of God. However, if you carelessly state you are blessed and really don't believe then you will lose the blessing and a curse of sickness will enter your body. Many people from the beginning of time until now have become sick with sin because of their lack of real devotion to the Word of God with careless conversation and not believing the Word. Your mouth can get you into trouble with God, because as I stated before the Word of God is living and breathing. In Hebrew 4:12, AMP says, "For the word of God is alive and active. Sharper than any double-edged sword, it penetrates even to dividing soul and spirit, joints and marrow; it judges the thoughts and attitudes of the heart". This is where wisdom comes into play you have to ask for wisdom and be careful of your thoughts and what you say. You cannot receive healing if you don't serve the living God and pretend to serve and don't believe. God knows your heart even if man does not know your real motives. You have to reach out and claim your healing and know that God's ways are not man's ways or thoughts. He is always ready to take you broken and full of sin. All you have to do is truly come with forgiveness in your heart and He will receive you to Himself and give you love and peace that you will never know in this world.

The Israelites discovered that God was patient with them after they left Egypt but He was very tired of their complaining and grumbling about going back to Egypt. It did not matter what miracles or how well the God of Abraham, Jacob, and Isaac took care of them in the wilderness there were the doubters and rebel rousers who kept the camp in constant confusion. This confusion came from Satan because he knew if he could continue the confusion and dysfunction then the Israelites would eventually kill themselves with sin and their wicked ways and salvation from the Lamb of God that was promised would not come to the world. What really saved the Israelites? It was the faith of Moses who constantly prayed for the people and the cleansing of the rabble rousers before they could enter the Promised Land. What do I mean by cleansing? Cleansing of sin from those who doubted that they could overtake the Amalekites - known as the Nephilim (the sons of Anak are part of the Nephilim) stated in Numbers 13:31-33 NKJV. Older Israelites from age 20 and up doubted God and Moses and were not allowed to see the Promised Land and possess it. Believing Israelites were born and learned the ways of God and they learned to obey and follow God for many years before Satan tricked the weaker believers and once again disobedience began. If it were not for God's grace and mercy no one would live and this is the miraculous ways of God and His boundless love for all mankind. For He looks out at His universe and blesses it daily and sees what we cannot see – He knows what we don't know and He loves us more than we could ever imagine in our earthly vessels that we possess. Once you know God Almighty, you will never turn back; but you will want to know how to get the healing of the Holy Spirit. Once you are able to "touch the hem of His garment", then you will become a whole person in Christ Jesus our Savior, who came to save us from our wretched sins. God is so amazing and full of love and once you understand that all God is - is pure LOVE; then you will be ready to take the journey to the edge of universe with Him and give praise an honor to His Son Jesus Christ. What a loving and un-tarnished sacrifice Jesus gave just for us. Think for a moment how much Jesus really loved us to undergo such harsh punishment before He was on the cross. He died such a horrific death just for us so that we could enter the Holy of Holies and be before the face of God Almighty when we die. Jesus died for every sin that was ever committed beginning with Adam and Eve until the end of the world. Take a moment and think about that (Selah). All of the most heinous crimes that could ever be committed - Jesus saw and knew every strike of the whip on His back, spit in His face, nails in His hands, slaps He felt, every lie told against Him and much more was for us. Just the thought of the cross should be enough for you to lay prostrate on the ground and worship God and ask forgiveness of your sins. If you don't feel this in your Spirit then you are not really part of Jesus Christ and your heart is hard. This is where you need to get to know Jesus and start reading the Word of God which is the Bible and ask for Jesus to come into your heart. It is a simple prayer out loud and immediately you will be saved. Healing only comes when you give your true body, Soul, and Spirit to God Almighty.

Hopefully this inspirational book will heal your weakened Soul and Spirit and change your unresponsive attitude about Jesus and serving Him as your King of Kings and Lord of Lords. For He is the only one that can save you and change this awful sin sick world we live in. Know that Jesus is coming sooner than you think and you need to be ready and know Him. Because if you don't it will be too late to come to know Him, because His Holy Spirit will be taken and hearts will grow colder and colder and thus rebellions will increase on this earth like you have never seen or experienced ever from now until the end comes. Get off the fence and get your life-less body ready to trust and love Jesus (Yeshua). Let the worldly things of this life go and get going with really falling in love with God and His Word. You will never regret your decision to become a solider in the fight for righteousness and love. It will not be easy being a true Christian. The Bible tells us that at least, you will be fighting for something that no one can ever take from you (Col 1:10, AMP). Your Soul and Spirit will be safe in the arms of Father God and His Son Jesus Christ. Alleluia!

## What are the Mere Edges of His Ways?

God's thoughts are not our thoughts. He says this in scripture "for my thoughts are not your thoughts, neither are your ways my ways," declares the Lord" (Isa 55:8, NIV). We only see what God wants us to see because; if HE gave us everything all at once we would be overwhelmed and would not know what to do. We would be so faint-hearted we would miss the blessings of Jehovah.

We only see and know a tiny edge of God's infinite wisdom and LOVE for us. As the scripture states in Job 26:14, NIV "the whisper we hear from God is a small voice that can only be heard clearly when we take time to read the WORD and commune with God in our silent prayer closet". When we really make time for the Father then we can appreciate the time we have with Him. Know we are growing every time we earnestly listen and wait for the Holy Spirit to speak to us. No wonder we are all confused with all the noisy sounds constantly bombarding and coming upon us daily. The enemy has large fiery arrows that are thrown at us constantly from the Lawless one, so we are in constant confusion and stress to the point we don't know what to do. This is when our faith starts to diminish. We rely on friends, family, or professionals to aide with our dilemma. Many of us just rely on ourselves because this is what we are accustomed to doing in the flesh. We think we have all of the answers and we don't. This is where immediate prayer should happen no matter what the devil is saying in your ear. You must keep on praying and quoting scripture then the devil will flee. You will defeat the devil because he does not want to hear the name of Jesus or constant scripture and will move on for a while. Now don't think this annoyance is over because the devil wants your Soul and Spirit. He will do everything in his power to entice you to sin and will be back soon with a vengeance.

For people who don't know Jesus this can be an undoubting task because fiery arrows are thrown at you constantly and you don't have a clue as to what is happening. The arrows represent the confusion, bickering, hate-full acts, lying, stealing, murder, un-ruly children, non-satisfaction on the job, bullying, un-explained or random acts of violence, etc. The Kingdom of God is needed and the arrows do not represent: Galatians 5:22, AMP "But the fruit of the Spirit is love, joy, peace, forbearance, kindness, goodness, faithfulness, gentleness, self-control. . . ". As a fence-sitting Christian or one seeking God you have to stop and look at your life and evaluate it and say "what is wrong with this picture"? If you see constant confusion and abuse then this is not God. Just because God allows these things to happen is not His fault. He has to allow the authorized sin to continue until the end when Jesus comes back and claims the earth and His own people. The "mere edge of God" is where God Almighty gave us the "free-will" to do as we pleased, but with a consequence as it was when Adam and Eve sinned for all of humanity. This sin was validated by Adam and Eve when they ate the forbidden fruit of the tree and gave permission to Satan to become the wicked protagonist of earth and all of mankind became shattered. No matter how God wanted to destroy man; after the fall of mankind, it could not be done without a Lamb that would come and save all of mankind by giving of His blood and taking upon Him all the sins of the world. You see the Triune God (God the Father, God the Son, and God the Holy Spirit) knew man would fall because Satan had been thrown out of Heaven for his pridefullness which became a flaw in his being. So Satan had a vendetta against God and in order to settle the score he sought to destroy God's magnificent creation because he wanted to be just like God. Jesus Christ is the one that could suffer for mankind and He alone was allowed to reclaim us and make us the righteousness of God. (Jn 3:16, AMP) "For God so loved the world that he gave his one and only Son, that whoever believes in him shall not perish but have eternal life". If you understand this concept then you are ready to except your Lord and Savior Jesus Christ. Accepting Jesus comes free but not without a cost and that cost is your obedience to His laws and concepts and learning to be free from sin.

We are in a constant whirlwind and battle for our very lives on a daily basis since the devil who wants to win you to his side will do whatever is necessary to get Christians and non-believers into his web of deceit. To break the power of the Lawless one, we should listen to the Holy Spirit "for if you live by its dictates, you will die". But if through the power of the Spirit you put to death the deeds of your sinful nature, you will live." (Rom 8:13, NLT). All you have to do is believe in Jesus Christ and you will be set free from all-unrighteousness. Jesus came to set the "captives free" not to bind them into more rules and regulations. The law is the 10 Commandments and the statues are the ceremonial/ordinances laws sent by God to Moses in the books of Numbers, Leviticus, and Deuteronomy. The ordinances are how you are supposed to treat one another on a daily basis; however, Jesus came and made these ordnances much simpler. In John 10:10, AMP, "The thief comes only to steal and kill and destroy; I have come that they may have life, and have it to the full". This is not to say the un-sinful way of living has been abolished but the New Testament made it simpler so that mankind would not be under the laws that were too strict to follow as the Jewish Pharisee and Sadducees had laid down for the people to follow.

How can we really obtain blamelessness? We can only receive true purity by asking Jesus to come into our heart. Then the Holy Spirit will come into your being and you will be one with God Almighty. "And the Holy Spirit helps us in our weakness" Romans 8:26, NLT. In Job 13:15, NKJV "God might kill me, but I have no other hope". We have the awesome LOVE of God who gives us the power to move and speak Life to our situations. In Luke 10:19, NKJV "Look, I have given you authority over all the power of the enemy, and you can walk among snakes and scorpions and crush them, nothing will injure you." Since we have already been given Power over the Lawless one, then we must "speak" the Words of Our Father and move on the prompting of the Holy Spirit (Hebrew Name for the God the Holy Spirit - Ruach HaKodesh). Scripture is full of the Almighty's awesomeness and love for man. This is the "mere edges of God" since He gives us the tools to successfully defeat the enemy, however; in our weakened sinful flesh we move to what is easier. We are accustomed to undertaking our own burdens, furthermore we ignore the prompting of the Holy Spirit which gives us the thoughts of God through the Holy Spirit who prompts us to stop sinning and listen to our Father. If we listen to the Father and this is a big if - then we will receive the message from our Lord through the Ruach HaKodesh (Holy Spirit). Consequently, we will have the correct guidance for our lives and will be sustained in righteousness. Our natural man will know life as we see it as "naturally like brute beasts" (Jude 1:10, NKJV) "speak evil of whatever" is not of the Almighty and this is not an easier life but a difficult one. Here is where our Lord and Savior Jesus Christ took our sins upon Him and becomes our advocate (God) to help us make the right decisions rather than our flesh which is being pulled into sin. This is only one aspect of the "edge of God". It would take volumes of books to really capture the awesomeness of God Almighty, but one thing I know for sure is that He is all you need to have a life that is full of joy that is unspeakable.

# What are the Words of God?

Do we as God's creation really know what God's words are? Do we really move on the prompting of the Holy Spirit? These questions have been answered so many times in books throughout the centuries. Yet we as the created creatures don't really know what or who God really is and how He wants us to act or speak.

The Holy Spirit is so involved with us until we don't know how to really let Him do his work in us as Christians, Messianic Christians, and Messianic Jews. We don't know our Spirit inside of us belongs to Almighty God. The true "essence" of the Spirit inside of man is the embodiment of God Almighty. "The spiritual person evaluates everything but is subject to no one else's evaluation (1 Col 2:15, NIV)." Scripture says, "But I say, walk by the Spirit, and you won't fulfill the lust of the flesh" (Gal 5:16, NIV)." For those who live according to the flesh set their minds on the things of the flesh, but those who live according to the Spirit, the things of the Spirit (Rom 8:5, NIV)." The Soul is the life of man, his character, intelligence, sight, hearing, speech, and emotions of Man and our flesh is the outward tent or covering over the body and the desires (Rom 13:14, MSG). There is a real reward to be transformed to righteousness through the Spirit who is inside of us. If we don't accept righteousness then there will always be a warring within ourselves. Paul the Apostle stated "I want to do what is good, but I don't. I don't want to do what is wrong, but I do it anyway (Rom 7:9, NLT)." No matter how we try under our own flesh we cannot do what is right but with Jesus Christ all things are possible and we can do what is right.

"Jesus looked at them and said, "With man this is impossible, but not with God. All things are possible with God." (Mk 10:27, NIV) We have buried our spiritual guide who resides inside of us. When we were created we let the Soul which is the flesh rule our whole being and then wondered why we are disappointed when we didn't get an answer from the Father. We are constantly disconnected with our whole being daily. This is why we cannot forget Father God is the Supreme Being who created everything in this world and not we ourselves. We must always remember God created us to have intimacy with Him. We can never forget the Creator has made us to have a relationship with Him. This spiritual intimacy has one purpose for mankind - which is to save more lives while we are on this earth rather than satisfy our own selfish desires. We must be mindful of our surroundings at all times and who we represent. We are children of the Most High God Almighty. No matter where our lives lead us we must be in touch with our Lord and Savior and let Him lead our lives; whether in a board meeting, school, in church, on a political journey, our homes, on the road driving, at a sports affair, musical concert, with our friends and many other ventures. You are the embodiment of Jesus Christ who constantly stated that we have to walk a different walk and conduct ourselves in the Light of God. Scripture states in Romans 12:2, NLT "Don't copy the behavior and customs of this world, but let God transform you into a new person by changing the way you think". There are so many verses in the Bible that describe who God really is and how He protects His own children and how the wicked will be banished from the earth or receive God's vengeance. Romans 12:9, NLT gives the perfect solution to any hateful act that is done to you, "Dear friends, never take revenge. Leave that to the righteous anger of God. For the Scriptures say, "I will take revenge; I will pay them back," says the LORD".  This is where you pray and ask God to forgive those who have wronged you and forgive them for they know not what they are doing as Jesus spoke on the cross as they Roman soldiers were casting lots on who would get His clothes.  How disgraceful this act was for the poor souls had no idea this was God in the flesh.  (Lk 23:34, NIV) "Jesus said, "Father, forgive them, for they do not know what they are doing." And they divided up his clothes by casting lots".

Psalm 34:15-22, NKJV gives hope to the hopeless and joy to the kindhearted man who knows that his Savior Jesus Christ will hear his prayers and protect him from all unrighteousness.

15 "The eyes of the LORD are on the righteous, and His ears are open to their cry.

16 The face of the LORD is against those who do evil, to cut off the remembrance of them from the earth.

17 The righteous cry out, and the LORD hears, and delivers them out of all their troubles.

18 The LORD is near to those who have a broken heart, and saves such as have a contrite spirit.

19 Many are the afflictions of the righteous; But the LORD delivers him out of them all.

20 He guards all his bones; not one of them is broken.

21 Evil shall slay the wicked, and those who hate the righteous shall be condemned.

22 The LORD redeems the soul of His servants, and none of those who trust in Him shall be condemned."

What a wonderful knowledge to know God will rush swiftly and save His own and give us courage, comfort, and strength where we fail in our earthly bodies.

## God's Words are "Silent, Loud, Kind, Passionate, Loving, Multi-Complex, and all Forgiving"

Did God not turn his back just once in all eternity on his Son so Jesus could fulfill the sin of humanity? Just think how awful this was for the Creator to have his Son go through the pain and anguish humanity sent him through just for mankind. This is the ultimate Love gift for mankind. Just take a moment and think about this statement. God so loved the world (and loved us so much) He sent His Son to save us of our sins and then had to turn His back on His own Son. So why did the Holy Father turn His back? As He cannot see sin or be a part of sin since Almighty God is HOLY and Perfect. This is what it means to be "beyond the edges of God" when you really think about the gift we have been given and yet we just throw it away daily. Our own selfish concerns of life are so important; God does not enter into the equation during the day or ever for some of us until we are suffering. Then we call on Him and then God becomes an "old shoe" (excuse the pun), we put on when it is convenient for us. Our Savior is not needed by us unless we can make earthly riches whereby we try to bargain with Almighty God. He is our creator and no bargains can ever be made. Eternity is the ultimate life to have with Almighty God. Since many folks don't care about their life in the hereafter, then they are missing out on the best God has for his children.

As we go through life, God's words float through every

breath we take and every second of our lives is like musical notes and we just go through life as if it is nothing. We really must think about who God really is. He is the Triune One who made our lives and the universe. We were created to love Jehovah and enjoy life with Him. This did not work out and Jehovah knew this plan of action when He created us. We are God's creation and our ancestors Adam and Eve had a choice to make when they sinned in the Garden of Eden. A wonderful gift was "free will" to choose to love and trust God or to trust our own desires. We have "free will" today and we exercise it daily. "Free will" should not be taken so haphazardly because Jesus the Messiah had to die for us. He gave everything for us to live either in sin or in righteousness. The only request Jesus made was for us - was to trust and obey the Word of God and to trust and love Him. Father God does not request we follow Him but just trust and believe in Him. It is so important we learn to trust God as this is the mystery of God's love for mankind. What a wonderful love God gives to us every second of every day. No human on this earth could ever give the love Adonai (God) gives to man. It does not matter what we do in our life, He loves us regardless up to our last breath on earth. He is willing to forgive us of our sins only if, we acknowledge He is Almighty God and ask for forgiveness of our sins with a repentant heart. You can have eternal life with the Triune God. One great example in the Bible is the thief on the cross asks Jesus to "remember me when You come in Your kingdom! And He said to him, truly I say to you, today you shall be with Me in Paradise (Lk 23:42-43, NKJV)." As you develop an understanding of the Word it is not complex it is so simple a child can understand. But why is it so hard for man to understand? Because he does not want to understand or believe in God and as far as many individuals believing in God, this is just a silly whim of the un-educated man to believe in anything but themselves. Prov 12:1, NKJV says the most profound statement "Whoever loves instruction loves knowledge, but he who hates correction is stupid". This statement says everything to the un-believer.

Now the Amplified Bible translation has a different twist on the "edge of God" verse; "Yet these are but [a small part of His doings] the outskirts of His ways or the mere fringes of His force, the faintest whisper of His voice! Who dares contemplate or who can understand the thunders of His full, magnificent power?

The translation of this verse really puts a new perspective on the underlining meaning. **First** of all, God's fiery force is fierce when it is necessary and is determined by God and not man. Man has played a role in changing the Almighty's mind about punishment. Moses changed God's mind when the children of Israel were worshiping the golden calf while Moses was on Mt. Sinai. In Exodus 32:14, NIV" Then the Lord relented and did not bring on his people the disaster he had threatened". God did not destroy the Hebrew people because of Moses and his earnest request and repentance for his people. "And when Moses saw that the people were unruly and unrestrained. . . "(for Aaron had let them get out of control, so that they were a derision and object of shame among their enemies)" (Ex 32:25, NKJV) it was God's grace and mercy which saved the Hebrew people. This is one example and there are many examples where a prophet, king, or apostle prayed and God listened therefore sparing disaster to mankind.

**Second**, God whispers as He did to Elijah when he escaped from Jezebel's death threats. Elijah ended up at a mountain where God asked him what you are doing here. "After the earthquake came a fire, but the Lord was not in the fire. And after the fire came a gentle whisper. And behold, a voice, a voice came to him and said, What are you doing here, Elijah? (1Kgs 19:12, NIV)." The gentle whisper was God's voice asking the prophet why was he fearful when he had defeated so many enemies of God. He forgot to pray when Jezebel gave her threat of death and this is a weakness in our flesh. This proves we are all vulnerable to the devil even when we have had a successful campaign with God and doing HIS will. This weakness lets us know all the people in the Bible are real just like us which is very refreshing. We have to make sure we have our armor on at all times because the devil is prowling around to see who he can kill, steal, and destroy daily.

**Third**, the magnificent power of God is very difficult for man to understand HIS awesome power. We will never understand God's power for HE is our Creator and His awesome mystery will be found in His Word. However, He does make it possible for us to know Him by studying, meditation, and reading His word. God reveals some of HIS awesome mysteries and secrets in HIS written Word such as in the book of Psalms, Job, Isaiah, Jeremiah, Micah, Revelation, and many other books in the Bible and Torah. One chapter in particular is Job 38 and 39 where God answers Job and asks him who made the universe "who determined the measures of the earth, if you know? Or who stretched the measuring line upon it? (Job 38:5, NIV)." These chapters provide an insightful mystery of God who made mankind.

God speaks through the words written in the Bible and the Torah whether we want to believe the written Word or not this is the message. We have missed the entire redemptive message by dividing ourselves into many different religious groups. These religious groups have caused confusion over the centuries making it difficult for the lost and confused to find their way to God. This has been the scheme of the devil to keep the Word of God from man and have him to continue to sin therefore having no redemptive qualities. Remember Satan wants to win this battle and he wants as many people on his side as possible and this includes confused Christians. Mankind has established so many precepts, laws, and religiosity it has made it so hard for God to break through and teach HIS very simple Word to his people. Let's not forget the false prophets that are numerous and have broken more would-be Christians than we can count. The seeking man just wants to find the truth but Satan and his tactical demons have been on the job before you can think clearly and they want to steer you away from the real truth and give you a false god to worship and that can come in many modes. For example: false TV ministers, evangelist, pop-up community church ministers, educated ministers who just learned the theology but never gave their heart and soul to Christ these are just a few examples. Then you have the occult church where they worship everything from sky, earth, animals, sun, moon, and wooden things that you can make with your hands. You cannot see or make God Almighty with your hands. But you see Him in everything that is in the universe because this is what He made millions of years ago. It is all good and beautiful even though we are destroying it at a rapid rate. It is still good what God has made for mankind.

Do we worship God? Or do we just "play" church and think it is enough to get you into heaven? Pretending to worship God in front of others and saying the correct "lingo" might get you into heaven. But being a "lazy" Christian is not enough for a real meaningful life for God. Besides, God is the ultimate judge and He will decide if your heart is right when you worship. He will determine if you are one of His sheep or not. If the Christian life were just to be "luke-warm" then why did Jesus have to come and save us? The WORD (which is Jesus the Messiah) has been with us from the very beginning of time. He has been with Adonai since the beginning of creation and so has Words of God, "Let there be Light" and there was light the moon and all of creation (Gen 1:3, NIV)." When God speaks it is like the sound of a ram's horn. When He speaks, life begins and moves throughout the universe. The spirals in the universe which are created daily are wonders to mankind. Scientists are actually discovering the complexity of the universe and the vastness of the universe is nothing compared to what God has waiting for Christians in eternity. For example the spiral shapes of the universe, our blood cells, our blood vessels, atoms, DNA; and all that makes us human beings were made by God. Just look at the temple in Jerusalem and how it is formed. There is the outer court, the inner court and the Holy of Holies. There are three parts to the Triune God – God The Father, God The Son, and God The Holy Ghost. A spiral formation has three parts known as the universe, which includes; planets, stars, galaxies, and the contents of intergalactic space. The great pyramids also have three parts. According to _Merriam-Webster Dictionary_ "a pyramid is a solid having a polygonal base, and triangular sides that meet in a point".[1] Would it be awesome to find out once we get to heaven and discover the great pyramid shape is the actual shape of the heavenly city? Now think about that. (Selah)

We were made from the spiral mass of the ground in the womb of the earth. This was how the first Man, Adam was made. This first operation was beautiful and full of love. For God wanted to have an intimate relationship with His creation. Father God was glad to have Man fill the earth - multiply until Man fell to sin which was made known to man by the devil.

Fire has always been a way God has shown He is near as it was with Moses at the burning bush. This observation of God's spoken Word comes from "fire is whirling" around in the universe. It has been suggested by theologians and historians - Mt. Sinai was a volcano. My personal thoughts on this theory is false, because the Hebrew people stayed in the area of Mt. Sinai for 40 years and there would be proof today if there was a volcano in archeological finding. If we believe the mountain was a volcano then we don't fully believe God. Let's not forget God is fire. To assume He did not sit down on the mountain and make fires come from a Burning Bush and a

---

[1] Merriam-Webster Collegiate Dictionary, 10th Edition, _pyramid_ definition, p952.

mountain with no trace of fire deposit is saying, Adonai is not our Creator and Father. Also the Bible and Torah would mention a volcano in the writings if this theory were true. Keep in mind the devil will distort the truth and send man on a side-ways journey to who knows where? Satan delights at our inconsistent thoughts he plants in our minds which should be supported by the Word of God the Holy Spirit.

Even if Mt. Sinai was a volcano just think how a volcano is made and how it erupts from a spiral mass. The mystery of how it is formed is amazing. A volcano can scream. This volcano mystery proves that everything in the universe praises God and can make a sound or praise God. This revelation makes the scripture "He replied, "If they kept quiet, the stones along the road would burst into cheers!"(Lk 19:40, NLT) the scripture is so true and complete. If we don't go out and preach the Word of God to the world during the - End Times then the very rocks of the earth will declare HIS glory.

One source suggests "We've known for a while earthquakes precede volcanic eruptions, but the new study showed as the eruption drew closer, the tremors' frequencies got higher and higher. When you speed up the data from the seismometer to make the tremors audible, it sounds like the mountain is screaming. Then, less than a minute before the eruption, the tremors suddenly stop. Who knew the hours before a volcano would erupt could be so eerie?[2] — By Colin Barras [Source MSN, 7/16/2013.

---

[2]Barras, Colin, "Volcano's scream may explain eruption's awesome power", News Scientist website, (2013,July,14)

What are the mere edges of Gods ways? Mankind has only seen a glimpse of Jehovah God in the scriptures. Unfortunately most individuals will never know Almighty God or experience real intimate love offered through Jesus Christ until they reach Heaven.  Scripture states there is only one way to Heaven and it is to believe in Jesus Christ the Son of God. Jesus Christ is the Son of God who - He died and was buried and rose from the grave on the third day and sits at the right hand of God Almighty in Heaven. (Rom 10:9, NIV) "If you declare with your mouth, "Jesus is Lord," and believe in your heart that God raised him from the dead, you will be saved." And also in (Matt10:32, NIV) "Whoever acknowledges me before others, I will also acknowledge before my Father in heaven." The faithful will see the glory of God Almighty and there is no word to describe the glory of God. It is apparent, I am writing in two different plurals but it is important to understand the "Edge of God". Since Christians are in the minority, it is more prevalent and with an urgency for Christians to spread the word of God. "Then we which are alive and remain shall be caught up together with them in the clouds, to meet the Lord in the air: and so shall we ever be with the Lord (1 Thess 4:17, KJV)."  Our time is short here on earth and the signs of Jesus Second Coming are all around us every day. We must watch and pray for the peace of Jerusalem since this is where Jesus left and where He will appear again.

If you can see the horizon on the ocean and think does it go farther?  Then you are correct.  As you travel toward the horizon it appears to keep moving until you reach your destination which in most cases will be land depending on your navigational path.

Would you be able to see the edge of the universe? Of course not, only God knows where the edge begins and ends. The point I want to make is mankind can imagine where the edge of the universe might be; but he will never find it because the edge is infinite.

The kingdom of God Almighty is explained plainly in the scriptures. "Only the righteous will get into heaven" (Matt 22:11-14, NIV)."

11. "But when the king came in to see the guests, he noticed a man there who was not wearing wedding clothes."

12. He asked, how did you get in here without wedding clothes, friend?' The man was speechless."

13. "Then the king told the attendants, 'Tie him hand and foot, and throw him outside, into the darkness, where there will be weeping and gnashing of teeth."

14. "For many are invited, but few are chosen."

Did it sound like someone tried to "sneak" into the Kingdom? With careful study you would think someone tried to come in with just works and no faith. The individual was not wearing the wedding clothes which meant they had not gone through the fire. They did as little as possible to advance the kingdom of Heaven on earth and thought they could buy their way into Heaven which is not how you get to the Kingdom. People often believe they can buy their way into the kingdom with their money or with works only. They believe if they give as little as possible for a tithe and join one or two organizations in the church or local organizations to help the needy this is all they need to do.  Non-repentant people still try to find short-cuts - keep on sinning without remorse and therefore think they can get into heaven.  Unless you repent of your sins and confess - Jesus the Messiah (Yeshua, HaMashiach) is your Lord before you die then you are doomed.  Even if a person who has committed the most heinous crime can find peace and enter the Kingdom of God, if they truly repent of their sins. Your repentant heart has to be truly heartfelt and real; believe me God knows your heart and He will know if your repentance is fake or real.  You must believe in Jesus Christ and ask for forgiveness.  Just as the thief on the cross asked Jesus to forgive him.  Then he was immediately saved and entered the kingdom.  (Lk 23:42, NIV)

In the scripture Matt 22:13, NIV Jesus made the point of telling the attendants (Angels) to tie the man who was not dressed in the wedding clothes and throw him outside into the darkness, where there will be weeping and gnashing of teeth. The place where the imposter was thrown was into the pit of hell.  The individuals who do not believe in the Triune God, thus having an un-repentant Soul will see the fires of Hell. How awful for them to live in fire and misery without the beauty and love of God for eternity.

Many Christians have the attitude once they get saved then this is all they have to do.  They think once they belong to a congregation it is like paying to get membership into an elite club.  Just pay the money or go to church every Sunday pay more monies and go home and forget what the minister spoke about in his/her sermon.  Take note: Heaven is an elite place but not a club.  You have to be born again with the Spirit of the Holy Ghost (Ruach HaKodesh) in order to really make changes in your life. You have to live a righteous life and have remorse for what you have done with sincere forgiveness which is displayed daily as you ask God for forgiveness of your sins. A "lukewarm" Christian will forget God is HOLY and pure with no sin. They will continue to live an unrighteous life after receiving the Holy Ghost and water emersion with no remorse. Our Heavenly Father is saddened by our actions of unrepentance yet He loves us just the same. This does not mean that you can continue to act cardinally without consequences. God will not have sin in Heaven or near His kingdom. God is Holy, perfect, and righteous. This is why HE sent HIS SON Jesus, to become the lamb to be sacrificed for our wretched sins. With the appearance of Jesus the Messiah on earth as the High Priest in the order of Melchizedek; (Gen 14:8-20, NIV) the daily sacraments which were done in the temple on high Holy days and festivals days were no longer needed. Ultimately, Jesus became the Lamb of God who bore all of our sins so that we could have an intimate relationship with God in Heaven as did Adam and Eve before the fall of mankind.

It is our responsibility to further the cause of Christ by changing our lives from being un-godly to an untarnished person that has found intimacy with Christ and has been changed from the inside out. Why is worship so important? God is not so multi-complex that we have to find excuses to worship Him. God is easy to love and He shows His love for us every second of the day. Without God's unconditional love we could not breath, move, get up, or even exist. The breath of God that was breathed into our nostrils is why we exist on this magnificent earth. Everything in creation worships God just look at the trees they grow up and so does all vegetation. Where does the air, water, and planets reside. They are up in the sky so we have to look up to see God this was all a part of the plan of creation. We know that Heaven is up and we know that Hell is down where we don't want to go. Even the devils in Hell have to look up to see God Almighty and cower at HIS brilliance. Lucifer was thrown from Heaven. How marvelous is our God. Why would you not want to worship the One who made you? You did not make yourself and you did not come from some mass in space that cannot be explained. Satan is just full of lies and he will tell them until he is put in his place in the bottomless pit of Hell when God comes back for judgement. The truth is God wins but Satan has no clue that he will lose this war with God Almighty. But, Satan will win those souls who don't worship Almighty God when given the chance to come before Christ before they die. Everyone will bow and then they will wish they had found Christ but it will be too late. There will be those demonic people who will bow down on their knees at the judgement, but will have no remorse no matter how hot the flames are going to be for them. How dreadful for the lost souls that will never know joy, happiness, and a victorious life with Father God and His Son Jesus. We as saints know that by worshiping we are putting the stamp of God in our hearts and pushing back Satan and his demons when we worship the Lamb of God who is the Son of God Almighty. When we worship we send a warning to Satan that he is not winning and Father Jesus is winning every time. Psalm 68:4-5, NIV is so glorious when it says, "Sing to God, sing in praise of his name, and extol him who rides on the clouds; rejoice before him - his name is the Lord. A father to the fatherless, a defender of widows, is God in his holy dwelling". How can you not worship God who is your defender and rides the clouds?

How excellent is your name Almighty God that you know everything before it is done. I am just amazed every time God works miracles in my life and I praise Him for everything daily many times. I know that every day I learn something new about the Almighty and it just blesses my soul to know I have a Father that is there all the time when friends, family, and loved ones are not there for comfort. Here is where the fence-Christian has to get off the fence and take stock of his/her life and stop giving excuses for not truly worshiping our Lord and Savior. There will come a time in everyone's life when you will have to make a choice who you worship. "But as for me and my household, we will serve the LORD (Josh 24:15, NIV)." The Psalms says, "The voice of the LORD divides the flames of fire. The voice of the LORD shakes the wilderness; The LORD shakes the Wilderness of Kadesh. The voice of the LORD makes the deer give birth, and strips the forests bare; And in His temple everyone says, Glory! The LORD sat *enthroned* at the Flood, and the LORD sits as King forever. The LORD will give strength to His people; The LORD will bless His people with peace (Ps 29:7-11, NKJV)."

Omnipresent God gives man a choice and our time is very short on this earth. All we have to do is look at the news and see all of the destruction that is all around us and know that we are coming to something dreadful very soon. You do not want to be left wondering what is going on because you did not make a choice to follow the living God who loves you more than you could ever imagine. Elijah the prophet went to the Israelites and said "How long will you waver between two opinions? If the LORD is God, follow him; but if Baal is God, follow him." But the people said nothing (1 Kgs 18:21, NIV)." Stand up and make a choice and get off the fence!

# Keep on Hearing and Do Not Understand

*Isaiah 6:9 "And He said "Go, and tell this people:*
*Keep on hearing, but do not understand; keep on*
*seeing, but do not perceive."*

We do not understand that God is just and He wants a relationship with us. What does this really mean? He wants to love us like no one has ever loved us. Our spiritual being is yearning for something more than we get from this life - we really don't know where to find the missing link. When we cannot get the love we need from this world then we look for love in all the wrong places this does not include looking to our Creator for love. Deuteronomy 31:6, NASB states, "Be strong and courageous, do not be afraid or tremble at them, for the Lord your God is the one who goes with you. He will not fail you or forsake you." Father God puts a wanting desire to seek Him out in our Spirit to search for Him which comes from the "pure" love God has for us. God's love is always there not like you get from mankind. Father God is present, just take time and listen to his "quiet voice" in our Spirit. However, a condition has to be met that is - you have to turn off all noise distractions around you. We can hear God's voice once we are tuned into the quietness around us. You have to tune your own mind into the stillness while you sit quietly and listen - otherwise your mind will tend to wander. Once you learn how to listen, then you can hear Him clearly within your Spirit. This will only occur if you are willing to listen to God in your everyday life. Connection with Jehovah is possible when you "ask" Him to "order your steps" (Ps 119: 133-136, KJV) ordering your life in everything you do.  It is a guarantee God will answer you, maybe not like you want, however; He knows what is best, because He created everything in the universe and your life will be in tune with what is righteous and His will. We must follow His ways.

What do we see with our eyes but never see with our hearts? Visualize for a moment a person who is visually impaired from birth.  They have a special sense to see the world in a different way than those who are sighted.  Those who have never seen the light of day will see nothing, because they have never seen anything. Suppose they had an operation that would give them sight then they would see blurry shadows and soon very bright lights. Finally they will be able to make-out shapes then see the world as sighted people see.  What a miracle to finally see what the visual world sees and how blessed that person will feel with gratitude to the doctors who operated.  Let's look at God's free gift of salvation through the eyes of Jesus.  We see our Lord Jesus Christ in everything that is created and we see the miracles that are created every day in our world from people being saved from one disaster to another. Before we knew Jesus we could see nothing very similar to a visually impaired person. Once we find Jesus then the light of God will enter our heart and we will see clearly the ways of God.  We must take time to read the Word of God or go to our place of worship to find out more about our Creator, who is just waiting for us to really SEE Him for who He really is, *Adonai* ("my Lord" in Hebrew). Christians have to look deep within their hearts and ask God to change the old person and become the new person that will be molded to a humble, kind, joyful, courageous, and loving person that can spread the Word of God. A Christian who has godly traits is a brave person and can take on whatever is sent their way. However, prayer is the major component to the success of a strong Christian. Once you are connected with the eyes of God then you can face any obstacle that the Devil will throw your way.

Have you ever taken the time to look up at the sky on a summer after-noon and really see the magnificence of God and appreciate the wonderment children see when they are looking up at the sky for the first time? It is truly amazing to watch flocks of birds dart across the massive sky and bathe in the beautiful sunlight of God Almighty. To watch the clouds move in after a beautiful blue sky has revealed a picturesque day the Lord has provided for mankind to experience. This image of beauty is something you cannot forget because it is the "mere edge of God". The creation of life on earth is stupendous and awesome it is almost beyond words. One has to stop and look up and just give praise to the Father for His marvelous creation of earth and beyond. Everywhere you look there is God, even the things man makes comes from God. If Father God had not given man the knowledge to make the things we have then we would have nothing. Mankind thinks he makes everything we have on earth, however; in reality there is another dimension hidden from mankind and it is with God. Heaven is so wonderful and awesome we cannot describe it. It is indescribable and Jesus speaks of the magnificent city, He is making for us who believe in Him. In John 14:3, NLT Jesus says, "When everything is ready, I will come and get you, so that you will always be with me where I am."

# CHAPTER 2

## How Small a Whisper We Hear of Him

Do you know you have all of the tools required to hear the voice of God? We are never tuned into God Spirit until we get into a situation which has taken us into the pit of despair, and then we call on God. Even if we are in tune to our Lord, we fail to hear Him talking to us in a "quiet whisper", because we let life's daily tasks take over our lives and many times we forget to pray and ask God to bless our existence. This is why the scripture (Job 26:14, NIV) states "And how small a whisper we hear of HIM." God does not speak in a booming voice but a whisper when speaking to us as an individual; just like the whisper Elijah heard from the mountain cliffs after running away from Jezebel. (1Kgs 19:12, KJV) "And after the earthquake a fire, but the Lord was not in the fire; and after the fire a still small voice." The Tanakh (Torah) version is somewhat different in the English language translation and contains in depth understanding to what the writer of scripture received from the Holy Spirit.

In verse 11, "And He said: "Go out and stand in the mountain before the Lord, Behold! The Lord passes, and a great and strong wind splitting mountains and shattering boulders before the Lord, but the Lord was not in the wind. And after the wind an earthquake-not in the earthquake was the Lord."

12."After the earthquake fire, not in the fire was the

Lord, and after the fire a still small sound."

13. "And as Elijah heard, he wrapped his face in his mantle, and he went out and stood at the entrance to the cave, and behold a voice came to him and said: "What are you doing here, Elijah?"

God spoke but it was a "small sound" again a voice but like a whisper. The Lord is like nothing we could ever imagine or comprehend because He is SPIRIT and HE has always been. This understanding of Adonai is far-reaching to our earthly minds even our Spiritual minds will not understand something until we are in heaven and we meet God Almighty face to face. Our Spiritual mind will comprehend the awesome power of Adonai when we give the Holy Spirit a chance to communicate with us through prayer and acknowledge the Holy Spirit exists. "But I tell you the truth, it is to your advantage that I go away; for if I do not go away, the Helper will not come to you; but if I go, I will send Him to you. And He, when He comes, will convict the world concerning sin and righteousness and judgment . . . "(Jn 16:7-8, NASB)". The magnificence and omnipresence of God is just overwhelming. Yet He loves each and every one of us with love flowing like a river never ending. "He who believes in Me, as the Scripture said, from his innermost being will flow rivers of living water. But this He spoke of the Spirit, whom those who believed in Him were to receive; for the Spirit was not yet given, because Jesus was not yet glorified (Jhn 7:38-39 – NASB)" We have no idea how much our Lord cares for us since most of us speculate about how we can get earthly possessions to satisfy the deepest longing of our heart. What a pity and a shame to love your creation so much and your creation will not acknowledge you exist. The Lord gave us the instructional manual which is the Bible, but we really don't follow the simple formula to peace, love, and everlasting life. (Josh 1:7-8, NIV) "Be strong and very courageous. Be careful to obey all the law my servant Moses gave you; do not turn from it to the right or to the left, that you may be successful wherever you go."

Romans 8:38-39, NIV "For I am convinced that neither death nor life, neither angels nor demons, neither the present nor the future, nor any powers, neither height nor depth, nor anything else in all creation, will be able to separate us from the love of God that is in Christ Jesus our Lord."

Galatians 5:22-26, NIV speaks of the living Life of the Holy Spirit which is how we must live and love one another. If we use these principals then we will hear the "small sound or whisper" of the Ruach HaKodesh (Holy Spirit which is the Hebrew translation) speak to us. Yeshua HaMashiach is indeed God the Son (Jesus the Messiah) speaking through the Holy Spirit. Galatians 5: 22-26, NIV "But when the Holy Spirit controls our lives he will produce this kind of fruit in us: love, joy, peace, patience, kindness, goodness, faithfulness, gentleness, and self-control; and here there is no conflict with Jewish laws. Those who belong to Christ have nailed their natural evil desires to his cross and crucified them there. If we are living now by the Holy Spirit's power, let us follow the Holy Spirit's leading in every part of our lives. Then we won't need to look for honors and popularity, which lead to jealousy and hard feelings."

God's love is pure unconditional and always the same today, yesterday, tomorrow, and into eternity. No one has power over us except God. Even if we don't believe in Adonai (God) He is in control of everything that happens no matter what it may be in this world. He is the actual key to power and the Holy Spirit is our guide for us in our troubles on earth.

The statement, "touch of Jesus garment" meant grace and mercy was given to the woman with the issue of blood, when she touched the hem of Jesus garment. Grace and Mercy is given to us daily as a gift from the Father. We have to reach out and believe and receive what God has given us already as children of God who believe in Him. The word "touch" transports an anointing to the believer from the inside out to the soul of man. At this point you have to really want to know Jesus Christ in order for Him to change your life. The "touch" is just the start of the miraculous healing for the believer. Once sinful man lets the Spirit man take over and stop listening to the flesh of man then the Soul and the Spirit can start to exist together in harmony rather than in conflict. Jesus wants to live inside of us and is waiting for us to turn over our lives to Him completely. So what does this mean? It means to surrender our day to day lives so we can run with success in our lives and without our Lord you will run alone in failure. When you are on the job, you think Jehovah is not going to know how to help you or listen to you. Your concept is incorrect, to think the Lord made you and left you on earth to figure out everything for yourself is a fallacy. God would not be loving or perfect, if He did this and this is *not* who He is. God made you and He knows every thought you will ever have in this life. He has provided you with your career, family, home, and substance of life. So why would He not know all answers and how to solve them for you. Your success and answers will not come to you as you think by your flesh or thoughts from your Soul, but by the Holy Spirit who imparts the words of God. God will often deposit the right words in someone's mouth for you in a conversation or through a scripture you have committed to memory. It is wise to memorize passages of scripture in your daily devotions then you will be equipped to handle attacks from the devil. Once you are truly connected to Jesus you will know when it is the Lord speaking or it is the devil giving you the wrong advice. Remember one way to test the spirit is to remember or read Galatians 5:22-23, NKJV " But the fruit of the Spirit is love, joy, peace, longsuffering, kindness, goodness, faithfulness, gentleness, self-control." If your thoughts don't line up with the scripture above then it is not from our Lord. Being a Christian is actually living the life God intended for us from the beginning of time.

For example, when your supervisor and colleagues curse and swear, talk about other folks on the job is when you stand your ground. Talk firmly let them know it is not appropriate talk and if they don't like it then know God is with you. It does help to say a quick prayer before you say anything, then you can be sure God is talking through you. You will be surprised how the conversation will change and how people will quickly walk away and forget the conversation. This is living the life God wants for us. The same principles apply in your home and family life. There will be moments where you will forget you are a Christian and you will act un-godly. Don't let this deter your connection to God just ask for forgiveness with a pure heart and God will forgive you. Remember the moment you find yourself failing to ask God to forgive you and put you back on track then you can fall into the devil's trap and spiral out of control.  Don't beat yourself up just keep pressing forward.  We all fall short in fulfilling God's best.  All He wants from us is to keep striving for the goal and trying and HE will do the rest.

You can lose anointing on your life if you greave the Holy Spirit, reject God or continue to be disobedient. You know when God has asked you to do something and you decide not to obey because your flesh says "buy this item now", or "I cannot obey God now because I am not ready or "it will interfere with my life right now".  You cannot wait any longer because Satan is in you and advising your flesh and giving "hints" and advice. You know God's voice and you reject Him because "you want what you want"!  When things don't work out then you cry out to God to help you get out of your mess. Many times God will not help you out of your mess right away. He wants you to see how your disobedience will send you straight to Satan and Hell fire. God wants you to really mean you are sorry and not pretend. Remember God knows all of your thoughts before you make them so He will know if you are sincere. Many times people are playing games with God or trying to make deals with him, as if He is the lottery or a game show host.  People just don't have a clue that Almighty God is GOD.  He is Alpha and Omega.  He has always been and will always be. Satan wants his throne so badly he has devised a parallel universe to duplicate what God does only it is for evil. Satan will not win.  His time is coming for the day of the Lord is coming sooner than later.

(Rev 12:9, NASB) "And the great dragon was thrown down, the serpent of old who is called the devil and Satan, who deceives the whole world; he was thrown down to the earth, and his angels were thrown down with him."

(Rev 20:10, NIV)" And the devil, who deceived them, was thrown into the lake of burning sulfur, where the beast and the false prophet had been thrown. They will be tormented day and night for ever and ever."

Satan and his army of fallen angels and many souls of mankind will fall into the trap of Satan. They will spend eternity burning in Hell and will never see the face of the Triune God. People will regret their decision but it will be too late to repent.

Have you ever sat down and had a wonderful day with wonderful thoughts? Then all of a sudden hateful thoughts about something that happened to you years ago are in your head. Something someone might have said about you or some kind of hateful act someone did to you? The hurtful thoughts will come out of nowhere during the course of the day; things you had forgot about will suddenly take center stage in your mind. You are now angry, hurt or ready to get even. These are not God's thoughts, but Satan trying to take over your mind. This is where you have to say "NO"; I am not thinking like this. Help me Holy Spirit. Holy God help me to remove these bad thoughts and then remember the Scripture says, "I can do all things though Christ who strengths me (Phil 4:13, NKJV)."

"The Sovereign Lord will wipe away tears from all faces; he will remove his people's disgrace from all the earth, The Lord has spoken it (Isa 15:8, NIV)." Jesus was the sacrificial

Lamb in place for us rather than an actual unblemished lamb was sacrificed at the temple. For God did not want any more sacrifice present on an altar since Jesus fulfilled this part of the plan of our redemption for us. What makes this so magnificent and loving is when you really realize Jesus was God in the form of man and He took on all scorn and sins for us; you cannot help but shed tears of joy and sorrow. It touches your inner Spirit and Soul to the point of tears to know someone loves you this much. He laid down His glory and came to earth to give us eternal life. He died, was buried, and arose with Glory to sit down at the right-hand of God the Father and took His place again with the Triune God is just miraculous. Just to know, He really is the creator of the world and He created You is enough to send you on your face and knees and worship God the Father, God the Son, and God the Holy Spirit. This revelation alone will make you worship like you have never worshiped before. You will turn your life completely over to Him with no fleshly thought, of being in control of your life, because you won't be in control any longer. The bizarre reality, you were never in control of your life ever! God was orchestrating your life all along; you thought you were in charge. God allows us to run along until we crash on the road. Then He sends angels to see if we are ready to commit to Him. The one thing is we only get so many chances before God lets us go headlong to destruction before you take your last breath. However it may be too late to speak and ask for forgiveness because you never know when you will take your last breath. The "touch of Jesus" garment is so important because what can we really do without His grace, mercy, and guidance? Nothing is done without God Almighty allowing things to happen whether it is good or bad. If bad things happen they are consequences of our sinful life.    We have to endure the anguish of pain which wrenches at our hearts. The Holy Spirit will guide us if we have confessed our love of God.    But those who do not know God will continue in their sin with no care to know their heavenly Father.  This is doleful for the sinner who knows nothing about God then rejects the only One who can truly help them.

## Let's Look At the Garment in a Different Way

God is and has always been. He is and will forever be the Creator of this Universe. His power will overthrow nations, kings, and all powers of this world. No one can overthrow the King of Kings and the Lord of Lords. The garment that Jesus wore was super charged with the essence of the Holy Spirit and His power as God the Son and Father on earth. Since He is a part of the Trinity, He has the same power that He had in Heaven. However, He did not use it as many expected. This made the garment more than ordinary but extraordinary. He set aside His true Glory to become human and experience our lives without sin. Jesus only used His divineness to heal the sick and to show man his faith in God which would bring him to a closer intimate relationship with the Father. The garment on the body of Jesus now modeled the "fire" of God the Holy Spirit that can only be released to those who really believe they can be healed. Many bystanders and Disciples touched Him daily as He passed by people on the road, but only the true believer who wanted a healing and thirst for healing received the gift. Only the ones with just enough faith "as a mustard seed" would receive the healing if they truly believed. This is why Jesus said "who touched me" because power left Him the "fire" from God the Father. (Matt 9:20-22, MSG) "And behold, a woman who had suffered from a discharge of blood for twelve years came up behind him and touched the fringe of his garment, for she said to herself, if I only touch his garment, I will be made well. Jesus turned, and seeing her he said, "Take heart, daughter; your faith has made you well." And instantly the woman was made well."

There was healing, grace, mercy, and power in His garments after Jesus was crucified. This is why so many claimed the garments had power and wanted to harness the power which could not be obtained by mankind. But the power was only for the real believer. The ones who were of the devil did not feel the power from the garments, but only a curse because their souls already belonged to Satan. Jesus came to set the "captives free" not to bind them therefore this is the truth of Jesus. Once Jesus was stripped of His garments then a separation of power happened and the garment still possessed the energy that was a part of Jesus, consequently a believer in God would feel the healing energy of the garment if they truly believed they could be healed. (Luke 4:18, NIV) Since God would not want man worshiping a material piece of cloth, the remnant garment lost its power once Jesus ascended into Heaven.

The omnipotent and omnipresent God is always with us; however we fail to see Him because we don't look beyond our own natural and physical image. We have deposited in our minds images from television, books, and photos from various paintings what Jesus would have looked like in the natural. We really don't know what He looked like when He was on earth. There is no photo of Him.

Touching God's garment in the Spirit will take the healing power from God to your Soul and Spirit. It will give healing to the one who earnestly searches to find Father God. Ask for repentance and believe in the Son of God. The act of searching and seeking to have a relationship with Jesus is a real willful act on the part of the seeker. When you look for God you will find He has always been with you. He just wanted you to have a true intimate relationship with Him and acknowledge Him. Once you reach out and actually touch God in the Spirit you will never be the same. You will become a changed person. To know God the Father, God the Son, and God the Holy Spirit will complete you as a person. All of your life, this act of love from God is what you have been seeking. The peace and love you will find from Him is like nothing you have ever experienced on this earth. This is why Jesus came, to "set the captives free from sin". All we need to do is believe (have faith) in Jesus the Son of God and we will be healed and set free from our sorrows, heartaches, and anguish. (Lk 4:18, NKJV) "The Spirit of the Lord is upon me; he has anointed me to tell the good news to the poor. He has sent me to announce release to the prisoners and recovery of sight to the blind, to set oppressed people free." Everything we do is from God. This is why He sent Jesus His Son, so we would learn to understand His will, way, statues, and commandments. Therefore we would learn to love each other as it was first intended before the fall of Man. We were made to worship the Trinity and to rule earth which He had made for Man. But instead, we gave away our inheritance to the devil and our perfect life on earth was cancelled. In the divine wisdom of Almighty God, He knew we would fail because the devil was already lurking around the universe waiting for the chance to fool God's creation. Remember, Adam and Eve had never experienced evil or deception before and they both fell hard because they had "free-will" to obey or disobey. The devil was successful. This is why the unstained garment of Jesus is so important. It represents the purity we welcome when we receive Jesus Christ as our Lord and Savior who will wipe away all tears from our eyes according to Isaiah 25:8, NIV "He will swallow up death forever". Therefore the power we receive from the touch of His garment will give us all of the healing for the world which is needed to pass on the message given by Jesus our Lord and Saviour.

There has been much speculation about a large piece of cloth known as the "Shroud of Turin". Could this piece of cloth possibly be the actual burial cloth of Jesus? This garment has not been proven to be the real burial cloth of Jesus. I tend to have an open opinion about the "Shroud of Turin" and consider that it might be the real cloth because no one has definitively dated the cloth, so it could really be the actual burial garment. After attending the exhibit in Michigan, I am quite sceptical to the evidence regarding the nationality and blood type found on the cloth. Jesus was born in the Mediterranean area where the blood type would have been type A due to the diet of the people and not type B. Jesus would have had a darker completion and curlier hair due to his Jewish nationality. Anthropologists have a tendency to make mistakes in their theory regarding ancestry especially for people in the Middle East. Would it be possible that God in all of His divinity would leave us a clue to His tormented anguish through a piece of burial cloth and thereby leave a photo image for mankind to find in the last days? I have had the pleasure to see the "Shroud of Turin" exhibit. One fact I observed from seeing the exhibit is no one has been able to decipher how the burned image of the man in the cloth got there. The actual blood stains from the beatings reveal so much blood on the cloth. The legs of the man had not been broken and the nails were pierced in the wrist. According to scripture and historical archeological data discovered during the Roman era; the feet had the nails in the correct place on the body  The blood stains on the cloth were so vivid one would know that the whip marks on the body were from the Roman soldiers beating the man. The leg image on the cloth was vivid and this person did not have their legs broken as was the custom during the time of Jesus crucifixion. The blood and water that came out of Jesus right side declared the redemption was complete and proclaimed the Deity of Jesus, the Messiah (Yeshua HaMashiach). Another observation is whoever this man was He rose upward through the cloth and left a complete three-D image of Himself. There is no doubt this was Jesus the Messiah. ". . . and to make plain to everyone the administration of this mystery, which for ages past was kept hidden in God, who created all things" (Ep 3:9, NIV)." Could this piece of cloth possibly be the actual burial cloth of Jesus? Yes, after seeing the "Shroud of Turin". I can definitely say it is possible that the cloth was the burial cloth for Jesus Christ our Lord. I do believe the true answer to how the cloth received the burned image will remain a secret until Christ comes.

Does this cloth have power? No, because it was only powerful during the time Jesus was on earth and wore the burial garment which covered His body.  After the ascension of Jesus the remnant garment had no power, but it is possible, Jesus might have left an imprint on the cloth so mankind would have some kind of physical proof He was on earth. Maybe this is why it is hard to date the cloth.  Even carbon dating has not actually confirmed the date of the cloth. This is a mystery and I believe will be a mystery for some years to come.

Did the disciples take the remnant garment or was it the Pharisees and Sadducees? I tend to think it was the Pharisees and Sadducees since they wanted to make other Jews believe Jesus was not the promised Messiah and He did not rise from the dead but was stolen by the disciples. Jesus was the promised Messiah even-though many of the temple priests did not believe in Jesus. Many Pharisees came into the knowledge to believe in Yeshua HaMashiach (Jesus the Messiah) before His death and after His death on the cross and resurrection. Satan was on duty to make an accusation and denial that Jesus had been raised from the grave so that many would fall into his trap and become his subjects. An article appeared in "Israel Today Magazine", April 2007, it mentioned the name of Rabbi Kaduri Yitzhak who wrote a note on a piece of paper and proclaimed Yehoshua, or Yeshua (Jesus), is the Messiah before he died and asked for it not be revealed until after his death. The Jewish Orthodox son of the Rabbi said it was not his father's handwriting and it was blasphemy to state that Jesus was the Messiah. People who were close to the Rabbi definitely said the handwriting was Rabbi Kaduri.[3]

(Matt 28:11-15, AMP)" While they were on their way, behold, some of the guards went into the city and reported to

---

[3] Schneider, Aviel. (2013, May, 30). The Rabbi, the Note and the Messiah article, retrieved from Israel Today News.

the chief priests everything that had occurred. And when they [the chief priests] had gathered with the elders and had consulted together, they gave a sufficient sum of money to the soldiers, And said, Tell people, His disciples came at night and stole Him away while we were sleeping. And if the governor hears of it, we will appease him and make you safe and free from trouble and care. So they took the money and did as they were instructed; and this story has been current among the Jews to the present day."

Just to make one more observation. The proof was in the sepulcher. The burial clothes undisturbed were the real proof. The Pharisees and Sadducees knew the truth but they did not want to lose power. Also God had blinded their eyes to see the truth so that the Gentiles could be saved and spread the word of God to the nations of the world. The LIE that was told became a believed LIE that was spread to the Hebrew people up to this very day in history. (Jn 20:4 -8, NKJV) "Both of them were running together, but the other disciple outran Peter and reached the tomb first. And stooping to look in, he saw the linen cloths lying there, but he did not go in. Then Simon Peter came, following him, and went into the tomb. He saw the linen cloths lying there, and the face cloth, which had been on Jesus' head, not lying with the linen cloths but folded up in a place by itself. Then the other disciple, who had reached the tomb, first, also went in, and he saw and believed".

## The Cloth

Let's look at the "Cloth" Jesus was wearing. It was spun sheep's wool comprised of one piece of material without seams. There was nothing special about it except for the tassels and the tallit which was the prayer shawl. It had a symbol on it that made it special for a Hebrew Rabbi. Num.15:37-40,NIV "And YHWH spake unto Moses, saying, Speak unto the children of Israel, and bid them that they make them fringes in the borders of their garments throughout their generations, and that they put upon the fringe of the borders a ribbon of blue: And it shall be unto you for a fringe, that ye may look upon it, and remember all the commandments of YHWH, and do them; and that ye seek not after your own heart and your own eyes, after which ye use to go a whoring: That ye may remember, and do all my commandments, and be holy unto your Elohim."(From the Torah)

The tassel fringe on the borders of the robe was what the woman with the issue of blood touched. A synagogue official came and bowed to Jesus and asked him to heal his daughter that had just died. In Matthew 9:19-20, NIV "and Yahusha (Jesus) arose, and followed him, and so did his disciples. And, behold, a woman, which was diseased with an issue of blood twelve years, came behind him, and touched the hem of his garment. Immediately she was healed and Jesus felt power leave HIM". So what was the power?

"You are the God who does wonders; you have

49

declared your strength among the peoples (Psalm 77:14, NKJV)."

"God has spoken once, twice I have heard this: that power belongs to God (Psalm 62:11, NKJV)."

"But our God is in heaven; He does whatever He pleases (Psalm 115:3, NKJV)."

God's power has always been. It is infinite. Since Jesus was God in the flesh then Jesus brought the power to heal with Him from Heaven. This is why He had to go away alone to rest and to pray to Elohim HaAv (God the Father). The power from God fills you with heat and love that cannot be described in human words, but you know the fire fills your Spirit and Soul. Power from God is warm and loving and you know something miraculous has happened to you that cannot be explained. Jesus is so wonderful He gives us unconditional love. We have no idea what powerful love can bring to your Spirit and your Soul. It is a fresh fulfilling all-consuming happiness that sends pure joy and love thorough out your entire being. This is what the woman felt that had the issue of blood. She knew if she would just touch the tassel on Jesus's garment then she would be healed. Just to touch any part of Jesus even his clothing would mean healing if you *truly* believed you could be healed. She had heard about Jesus and knew he had healed many in the surrounding area. She had been suffering from a hemorrhage for twelve years but, after touching the fringe of Jesus garments she was made whole and the bleeding stopped. What a blessing and a testament she had for others who had weak flesh.

# CHAPTER 3

## The Touch of His Garment

Sing to God, sing in praise of his name, and extol him who rides on the clouds; rejoice before him-his name is the LORD. (Psalm 68:4, NIV)

The woman who touched Jesus could only give "praise to the Lord, the God of Israel" (v.68) because the infirmity she had for 12 years was gone. This is a miracle because to be healed immediately is a gift from God. But it is also breathtaking to know "just a touch" of the fringe on the bottom of Jesus's garment allowed the woman to be completely healed.

A lesson can be learned about this event. If we as mankind all believe in the Son of God, then we too can be healed of everything. Just like Jesus said to the woman at the well, "Everyone who drinks this water will be thirsty again, but whoever drinks the water I give them will never thirst. Indeed, the water I give them will become in them a spring of water welling up to eternal life (John 4:14, NIV)." This revelation was hard for me to understand at first, but I truly understand the significance of this phase in my life. You must look deep within yourself and find the meaning of the "water" the purity of living the life God ordained us to live without sin and remain faithful and not sin daily and have the forethought to think there would not be any consequences from your sin. Water represents the purity and cleansing in your life, if you just give Jesus a chance to give you fulfillment in your life and not the "earthly things" then we will receive the cleansing from the Father. For example, new electronics, clothes, vacations, new house, new friends, new relationships, and a new job will prove to be of no significance without God. You will feel like the woman with the issue of blood bleeding internally and trying to find an answer. The only fulfillment is God. When you truly turn your life over to God then you are truly fulfilled with the life of healing and purity of God in your spirit every day. You want to praise God and know everything in the universe is ultimately praising God because it is lifting up toward Heaven.

# Keeping Your Focus

We forget God knows everything about us. This is why it difficult for Sinners and Christians to acknowledge and retain their focus on righteousness. Whatever we do God knows everything. The secular side of this scenario deals with believing in fairy-tails presented early in some of our lives. We can believe in Santa Clause, Easter Bunny the "naughty and nice" and believe that Santa can see everything. Santa is really a falsehood presented to society to entice parents to buy gifts for their children. However, after we come of age to know the truth about this fairy tale then we are comforted knowing the falsehood is the best kept secret. So, if we can believe the LIE about fairy tales then why can't we believe God made us and has many eyes and knows our true heart? "Nothing in all creation is hidden from God's sight. Everything is uncovered and lay bare before the eyes of him to whom we must give account". (Heb 4:13, NIV) and "The eyes of the LORD are everywhere, keeping watch on the wicked and the good (Prov 15:3, NIV)." God knows what we are thinking and feeling before we do anything then we should be able to believe God only wants the best for us and yet we don't want to believe in Him? The omnipresence and omniscience of Holy God is eternal and everlasting and this pretense that we have come to believe that earthly idols (Santa Clause, Easter Bunny, Halloween, i.e.) is not real; but, a way to keep our minds off Christ and on to the devilish things of this wicked world. We need to keep our focus on the power and healing of God as the touch of his garment has led many to believe in

God incarnate. Such belief will eventually lead us all; to the revelation we cannot live without God. HE is our all in all.

What kind of garment did Jesus wear? In John 19:23, NIV says Jesus wore 4 other garments apparently and the scripture affirms: "When the soldiers crucified Jesus, they took his clothes, dividing them into four shares, one for each of them, with the undergarment remaining. This garment was seamless, woven in one piece from top to bottom."

While Jesus was on earth he would have worn wool garments like other Rabbi Priests. He would have had 4 tassels or fringe on His garment as well. Many Gentiles and Jews believed the Messiah would have power to set them free. The garments Jesus wore had tassels and a woman with a bleeding disease believed Jesus was the Messiah because she reached out and touched his garment and by doing this Jesus said to her "Daughter, your faith has healed you. Go in peace and be freed from your suffering . . . (Mark 5:34, NIV)."

I particularly enjoy Matthew's writings in Matt 8:3, NIV. Where he explained and revealed God's true heart in the verse. "Jesus reached out his hand and touched the man." I am willing," he said. "Be clean!" Immediately he was cleansed of his leprosy". Notice that immediately the man was cleaned (healed) of leprosy because he was willing to be healed and Jesus told him not to tell anyone. But as you know, if you want something repeated say "do not tell anyone" and believe me it will be everywhere in minutes. This is how the gospel of Jesus Christ was spread so quickly because the former leprosy man went to the Priest and I am sure on the way he saw many who knew he was now clean rather than "un-clean" and his gratification was jubilant. Another favorite parable is in Matt 8: 5-10, NIV, it tells of the centurion who had a sick servant boy but did not want Jesus to come to his home. He had so much faith that all he needed from Jesus was just a word that his servant was healed. "Lord, I am not worthy *or* fit to have You come under my roof; but only speak the word, and my servant boy will be cured (v.8)." Jesus was marveled by the faith of the Roman centurion because he was over many men in the army and believed if he told them to go they would go and do as they were instructed to do. Jesus replied "I tell you truly, I have not found so much faith as this - with anyone, even in Israel (v.10)." What a wonderful faith statement from Jesus to say about the Gentile centurion. Believing and trusting Jesus Christ is all we have to do and know if we have faith as small a mustard seed you can be saved by the blood of Jesus Christ (Matt 17:6).

In Job 26:14, NIV the fearsome voice of God is just a *whisper*, but God's magnificent power and awesomeness as our omnipresence and omniscient God displays His true love of mankind and His ultimate love is to have a true relationship with His creation. As human's beings, who can really understand and comprehend WHO Almighty God really is and His awesome power? All we have to do is look up and see the beauty in the heavens. Look on the earth the trees, flowers, animals and just the miracle of birth alone is a wonderful phenomenon and the loving Father God shows his awesomeness in so many ways. To create and make the world and all of the beasts that live on earth is overwhelming if you really think about it from a biblical or even a scientific perspective. The creation of the entire universe is beyond anything we can ever in this life time comprehend and truly understand because it is so vast and always changing. So you have to have faith to know the breath of God is the wind that surrounds the earth. He spoke the world into existence and the heavens became the firmament we know today. Genesis 1:21-22, NIV) states; "In the beginning God created the heavens and the earth. The earth was formless and void, and darkness was over the surface of the deep, and the Spirit of God was moving over the surface of the waters. . . " that scripture statement is enough to make you fall to your knees and pray and cry out to our maker the one who made us. Everyone on earth has some kind of god they worship. Whether it is Almighty God, idols, or things they have in their possessions they are meaningless - although from the scripture, it is clear there is only One God and He is God Almighty or in Hebrew He is known as, YHWH the un-spoken name of God.

Job 26:5-14, Amplified Bible (AMP)

5. "The shades of the dead tremble underneath the waters and their inhabitants".

6. "Sheol (the place of the dead) is naked before God, and Abaddon (the place of destruction) has no covering [from His eyes".

7. He it is Who spreads out the northern skies over emptiness and hangs the earth upon or over nothing."

8. "He holds the waters bound in His clouds [which otherwise would spill on earth all at once], and the cloud is not rent under them."

9. "He covers the face of His throne and spreads over it His cloud."

10. "He has placed an enclosing limit [the horizon] upon the waters at the boundary between light and darkness."

11. "The pillars of the heavens tremble and are astonished at His rebuke."

12. "He stills or stirs up the sea by His power, and by His understanding He smites proud Rahab". (The dragon/ devil)

13. "By His breath the heavens are garnished; His hand pierced the [swiftly] fleeing serpent".

14. "Yet these are but [a small part of His doings] the outskirts of His ways or the mere fringes of His force, the faintest whisper of His voice! Who dares contemplate or who can understand the thunders of His full, magnificent power?"

(Job 26:7, NIV) For thousands of years various theories of what mass really supports the earth - elephants, giants, and other fantastic means - were accepted by mankind as truth. The Bible made no such absurd error. How could Job, more than 3,000 years ago, possibly have known that God "hangs the earth upon or over nothing," except by divine inspiration?

(Job 26:14, NLT) "These are just the beginning of all that he does, merely a whisper of his power. Who, then, can comprehend the thunder of his power?"

The amplified bible version is my favorite because it entices you to other thought processes that you might not have acquired through the Holy Spirit if you only sought out one translation. This is why I like reading and studying more than one translation and especially reading the Torah, you can get a totally different perspective of God and His awesomeness. Words in the Bible have more than one meaning especially in the Hebrew language. Since the first five books of the Bible (Torah) were written by Moses it was written in Hebrew so the language of God is Hebrew a language we should study and learn. If we study the Word then you will start to have an intimate relationship with God Almighty.

(Job 26:14, AMP)"Yet these are but [a small part of His doings] the outskirts of His ways or the mere fringes of His force, the faintest whisper of His voice! Who dares contemplate or who can understand the thunders of His full, magnificent power?"[4]

In the verse "the faintest whisper of HIS voice" is so loving and comforting to my Soul and Spirit. God's whisper is soft and soothing to my Spirit and we just have to get quiet and listen to His voice. Jesus does whisper in our minds when we are awake, asleep, praying or when we are in an actual visionary state. The fear of the Lord is frightening and at the same time loving because God gave His Son Jesus to mankind so we could be transformed into the righteousness of Jesus. We should become the people that will someday reign and rule with Jesus on the earth after our transformation to the immortal bodies that will never die, feel pain, and anguish again. How would Job know how the throne of God hung in the heavens unless God revealed everything to Job? As a follower of Jesus

---

[4] "The Book of Job is believed to the oldest book in the bible, while scholars believe it was written as late as the time of the Babylonian exile. Job, Moses, and Solomon have been suggested as possible authors."

Christ, you have to think beyond what you see and read with understanding to know when Adam and Eve were created God already saw the world with it frailties. He saw the fall from Abraham, Isaac, Jacob, Moses, Elijah, all the prophets the fall of the Hebrew people, Jesus coming to save mankind to the crusades, the Holocaust, and Israel becoming a nation. He also saw America becoming a sanctuary for all peoples of religious backgrounds to the present day and future prophetic events. He knew we would be martyred and would one day in America have to give our lives for His sake and we must stand-up and declare our faith to Jesus Christ or we will die in our Spirit and we will never see the face of God. The Triune God see's the very end of time and the conclusion of life as we know it. The Bible has already foretold the end and who will win in the end and that is Almighty God! Just pause for a moment and think about this statement. We are so blessed and we don't even regard our breath we take every second as a gift from our Creator.

## Wellness in Your Spirit

You must be well in your spirit in order to hear the word of God. God's words are "alive" and they are still in the universe giving Life to everyone who will listen and obey. God is our Father but He wants everyone to enter into the gates of heaven and he does not want everyone to go to Hell. Regardless of what you might have been taught in your life by family, friends, and various men of the cloth. God is a forgiving God and He only wants the best for us, because He has unconditional Love for us that never changes beyond our breath. Even the most hideous crime committed, God will forgive the person if they truly _ask_ in their heart for forgiveness and live a life of righteousness. What does this mean for people who ask for forgiveness with their last breath? The thief on the cross did ask Jesus to "remember me when you come into your kingdom" he did ask and was forgiven. This is all the proof we need to prove forgiveness with your last breath. There is a caveat before you receive forgiveness you would have to be _alive_ at the moment you ask for forgiveness. The opportunity is not a <u>Guarantee</u> - you will have time to ask God to forgive you. This is why you must be a part of the kingdom of God before your time of death.

Luke 23:39-43, MSG" one of the criminals hanging alongside cursed him: Some Messiah you are! Save yourself! Save us!" But the other one made him shut up: Have you no fear of God? You're getting the same as him. We deserve this, but not him—he did nothing to deserve this. Then he said,

Jesus, remember me when you enter your kingdom. He said, "Don't worry, I will. Today you will join me in paradise."

Does this mean the person went to heaven after living a life of crime? The answer is yes. Why did God forgive him? First the repentant thief was alive and second he was truly sorry for his crimes which he spoke so eloquently to the non-repentant thief as he chastised him. This is the real meaning of forgiveness. _You have to have a repentant heart and fear God at the same time._ You cannot fool God He knows your heart and that will never change because He made us and He knows everything about us. If a person states he is sorry, but does not really mean it in their heart they are only fooling themselves because God cannot be deceived by man. "Don't be misled: You can never make a fool out of God. Whatever you plant is what you'll harvest (Galatians 6:7, MSG)." The original translation states: "Be not deceived; God is not mocked: for whatever a man sows, that shall he also reap."(Gal 6:7, KJV) Many people try to fool themselves into believing they can bargain or slip under God's watchful eyes and pretend to repent then go back to sinning with no consequences. However, God knows everything and in His divine wisdom He is waiting for them to really repent because He loves them, but if they don't repent then they will go to their earthly father who will torment them for an eternity.

The Spirit of God dwells in his anointed children and He walks and talks with those children who truly want to have an intimate relationship with Him. We all fail to have a relationship with the heavenly Father because, we are fooled by life's cares and this is just what Satan wants and strives to put into our Soul and Spirit daily.  If Satan can keep our minds off God (the Holy Trinity) and keep our minds on mindless things of this world such as; jobs, food, clothes, our electronic gadgets, TV, the next reality TV show, and social media then we are doomed.  Yes we all have to work and eat but God will provide those things for us, we do not have to worship these things.  Some other examples are: scheming to get ahead or lying on job applications so we look good until we are found out. We have to have the latest in clothes because this is what society says you have to have or to look like some Hollywood star instead of being ourselves. Even our eating habits are part of the scheme to derail us; so we have health concerns because we eat the wrong kinds of foods.   Therefore we are sick and cannot do the work of Jesus by spreading the Word because now we are only concerned about ourselves.

These are all lies of the devil and his minions and he will gladly keep you so busy you forget to pray and read your bible.  You even forget to go to church until you are so far out of touch you cannot see your way back. Then guilt sets in and your Spirit is dry and parched from not having the love from God.  You can get God's love back quickly, just call on Jesus (Yeshua) the son of God and he will help you come back to the loving arms of God.  Matt 4:4, NKJV "But He answering said, It is written, Man shall not live by bread alone, but by every word which proceeds out through God's mouth."  This statement is so powerful.  It lets you know God is all Power and Glory.  The Almighty does not need mere humans to validate anything that is said or done on this earth because He is "I AM THAT I AM". The Almighty God's words are living every second of every day and we must learn to listen and obey.   The greatest statement in this scripture "goes out through God's mouth" lets us know God is real and we are made in His image. God has a mouth so we should obey what he says. The best way to get to know God is to read His Word. He reveals himself through the scriptures. He has all of the emotions we have and yet he is PERFECT and loving for his wonderful creation. He loves us because He made us. Just as we want the best for our children and families He wants to best for his children.

We can try everything to satisfy our empty longing to be truly happy. However true happiness only comes when we finally give our entire Spirit to the Almighty and let Him show us what real life on earth is supposed to be. Now don't get me wrong the bible clearly states we will have trouble.

John 16:33, AMP,"I have told you these things, so that in Me you may have [perfect] peace and confidence. In the world you have tribulation and trials and distress and frustration; but be of good cheer [take courage; be confident, certain, undaunted]! For I have overcome the world. I have deprived it of power to harm you and have conquered it for you."

Our Creator has made a provision for us to get out and be free in our Spirit and know that whatever comes He will be there to see, help, assist, carry, and if necessary pull us through the storms of life. In Luke 15:24, KJV "For this my son was dead, and is alive again; he was lost, and is found . . . "

What really does the Spirit do? Now the Spirit can

become evil if it is not connected to God. In Zech 12:1, NLT 'This message is from the Lord, who stretched out the heavens, laid the foundations of the earth, and formed the human spirit." This is where the Holy Spirit resides inside of everyone when you become a Christian. You know right and wrong and your Spirit gives you promptings. It is prevalent in your Spirit once you become a Christian. "Whoever has the Son has life; whoever does not have the Son of God does not have life." (1John 5:12, NIV) also in Ephesians 2:1-8, KJV," And you hath he quickened, who were dead in trespasses and sins; Wherein in time past ye walked according to the course of this world, according to the prince of the power of the air, the spirit that now worketh in the children of disobedience: Among whom also we all had our conversation in times past in the lusts of our flesh, fulfilling the desires of the flesh and of the mind; and were by nature the children of wrath, even as others. But God, who is rich in mercy, for his great love wherewith he loved us, Even when we were dead in sins, hath quickened us together with Christ, (by grace ye are saved;) And hath raised us up together, and made us sit together in heavenly places in Christ Jesus: That in the ages to come he might shew the exceeding riches of his grace in his kindness toward us through Christ Jesus. For by grace are ye saved through faith; and that not of yourselves: it is the gift of God. . . "

In the word of God the Bible teaches that man imparts certain aspects of the human mind, including self-awareness, intellect, creativity, personality and temperament - everything that enables human accomplishment and knowledge short of true spiritual understanding (1 Cor:2:11, NIV). The Sprit of man returns to God upon death. (Ecc 12:7, MSG) "The body dust will go back to the earth, returning to what it was, and the spirit will return to the God who gave it." This verse clearly states the Spirit and the Soul will return to its creator. The believer in Jesus Christ has a wonderful reward when they die, to be with God Almighty forever. The Bible tells us after death believer's Souls and Spirits are taken to heaven, because their sins are forgiven by having received Christ as their Savior (John 3:16, 18, 36, NIV). For believers, death is to be "away from the body and at home with the Lord (2 Corinthians 5:6-8; Philippians 1:23, NIV)." What a fantastic connection to God and to know once you are connected with the Creator then you can live with Him forever in Heaven. Unfortunately, the opposite demise is given to an un-believer. There is another reality and it is to live without the Love of Jesus Christ and to be damned for an eternity. To burn in the lake of fire for all of eternity away from the face of God is the most heart wrenching event that could happen to a person. Those individuals who let the schemes of the devil deceive them for all of their mortal life will regret their decision not to follow Jesus the Messiah. Once an un-repentant Soul dies they cannot change their destination. For a believer in Jesus Christ, it appears that while the Souls and Spirits of believers go to be with Christ immediately after death, the physical body remains in the grave "sleeping." At the resurrection of believers, the physical body is resurrected, glorified, and then reunited with the Soul and Spirit. This reunion and glorified body-soul-spirit will be the possession of believers for eternity in the new heavens and new earth (Revelation 21-22, NIV). What a wonderful and loving promise to have from Jesus Christ to know life continues immediately after death in the arms of Jesus.

For unbelievers, they are sent immediately to a temporary holding place called Hell, to await their final resurrection, judgment, and eternal destiny. Luke 16:22-23, NIV describes a rich man being tormented immediately after death and he was in hell. This busy individual had too much and his businesses were more important than helping a poor beggar. He could not stop and offer help to the poor beggar because this was beneath him. We see people every day begging for food and of course we cannot give to everyone and especially these days when you really don't know if danger abounds around the corner from helping your brother or sister; but, pray quickly and God will give you wisdom on what to do. Self-absorption is not a picture of a Christian however, we should move to help when appropriate and give back to those in need, when someone has lost a home from a fire, tragic accident, monies for burial of a love one, food and clothing for the needy, i.e. and I could go on. There are so many good people in the world helping but not all of them are Christian but have good hearts and these folks need someone to help them complete the process to the Cross of Christ. This is where the fence Christian can become effective and get going with their lives and stop waiting for someone else to do the work that they could do. We do not get to Heaven on our works, but by the Blood of Jesus the belief and faith of Jesus the Son of God. Yes, you can get to Heaven just by being saved but there is so much more to do before Christ will come and why would you just want to do minimal work? God Almighty is so much more and to really get to know Him you have to get up seek the Lord with 100% of your being.

Otherwise you are lying to yourself and the Father God about your involvement with Him. You do not want to wake up one day and find yourself looking up to Heaven and regretting your decision not to complete your burning desire to know God. The poor beggar went to Heaven and the rich man went to Hell.

# Just the Edge of God

Psalm 2:5-6, AMP, "He speaks to them in His deep anger and troubles (terrifies and confounds) them in His displeasure and fury, saying, yet have I anointed (installed and placed) My King [firmly] on My holy hill of Zion."

The many facets of God are truly displayed in verse 5 and 6 where God speaks with his deep anger whereby he terrifies and confounds the unrighteous. They have no idea the day of wrath is upon them since they are going about doing their evil as they always have with no care to be obedient. They do not know Jesus the Anointed One, even though He has been here and preached over 2,000 thousand years ago. Evidence of his arrival is on the holy hill in Jerusalem however, many un-believers still mock and persecute the righteous sons of God.

God is a vengeful God. He will not let the unrighteous continue to persecute his own for long without striking the enemies of the devil. In Psalm 3:7, AMP "Arise, O Lord; save me, O my God! For You have struck all my enemies on the cheek; You have broken the teeth of the un-Godly." God has struck down the enemies of the righteous and will always protect His own.

Almighty God (El Shaddai) means the destroyer comes from on high. The root word "shadad" means to overpower" or "to destroy".

God will not be mocked and He will destroy if you are not forthcoming. In the Old Testament God destroyed the Hebrews and their enemies many times in order to bring the Hebrews back to Him so they would worship and have a relationship with Him as was promised. Pure reconciliation to God only happened after many trials and disconnects from the Almighty and 40 years of wandering in the wilderness. Even after the 40 years, the Hebrew people would sin again. God would forgive them and they would sin again and God would forgive once more. This Love from God has continued up to this very time period in history. This lets you know God is a loving and forgiving God and His dedication and commitment to mankind is eternal because, of His boundless love for His creation. Matthew stated, "All of you must keep awake (give strict attention, be cautious and active) and watch and pray, that you may not come into temptation. The spirit indeed is willing, but the flesh is weak Matt 26:41, (AMP)."

We only know what the Bible tells us in the vernacular but in order to really start to understand and know God you have to mediate day and night and pray for wisdom and understanding. After meditation and prayer you will start to understand the wisdom (the edge) of God. There are three things you have to do:

1. *Pray*, 2. *Read the scripture*, and 3. *Do what it says*, in order for your Spirit and Soul to finally understand they have to work together so that you will become the person God wants you to be. Psalm 1:2, AMP says "But his delight and desire are in the law of the Lord, and on His law (the precepts, the instructions, the teachings of God) he habitually meditates

(ponders and studies) by day and by night." Only when man has fully understood this verse and he actually starts to do what it says will true wisdom and understanding come to the reader. The WORD of God is "Living" it is not just a book but an inspired book that was given to the disciples and our ancient forefathers by God and the Holy Spirit for us to learn and follow God (2Tim 3:16, NIV). We are blessed to have the written word. We can read it for ourselves and come to an understanding of what the scriptural text means. The Israelites did not have the written word they had the Torah that was read to them by the Rabbi during the time of Jesus. It was not until much later in time when we had the first Bible (Gutenberg Bible) that was printed in 1454 or 1455 that the Word was starting to spread via printed material. The Torah was the only document having the written language transcribed by a Scribe onto parchment paper in the Hebrew language. Prior to the printing of the first Bible and Torah everything was recited. The Bible was not circulated world-wide until the1800's and only the elite could read. However, once people through-out the world learned to read then the various translations of the Bible were written and people from all lands started to get the written word. We can go to any online or brick and mortar store to buy a Bible in our wonderful country. There are still countries that will not allow the Bible to be read and people who do not know the Word. This is why we must press forward and spread the Word quickly because time is so short and the Lord is coming back in a "second of time" whether you choose to believe it or not. The signs of God's coming is everywhere in the world. Stay prayerful and obedient to Almighty God and he will protect and save you in the time of distress which is coming.

"The edge of where God is and where His blessings start is miraculous because God looks at every detail and not just the big item (Matt 2:15, 13:35, and John 19:24, 28, NKJV)."

The verses describe God's awesomeness and what He has made and created. Man has done nothing by his hands without God giving man the knowledge and inspiration to make things. The previous verses describe creation of the earth and God asks Job what have you made with your hands? In verse 14 "how faint the whisper we hear of Him!" After all of the loud creation discourse there is still the small whisper of God that is so prevalent in the ear of the believer.

God wants all of his children to know who He really is and to know that everything we have has been created for us to enjoy on this earth. We are to enjoy life through God's loving hand and not forget about God. When we start to worship the things of the earth and stop worshipping God then we are into sin and idol worship. "Who can endure the day of His coming? (Malachi 3:2, NIV)." No one can endure the Lord's fiery appearance when He returns to judge the earth. Yet we think that we can "run" or fight God who is the Creator of the universe and us. We don't want to believe in God and just as soon as something peaks our interest and looks good to our eyes we are on to anything but holiness. Those earthly materialist things we idolize will send us straight to Hell. This is why is it important to "touch" the hem of Jesus's garment who is the Son of God. Allow the Master to flow though us and not the deceiver who is Satan. The deceiver stands waiting and taunting us to do wrong. Satan does not care as long as he can plant ungodly thoughts in our minds. Then he knows that soon our minds will go back to the wrong things unless we are constantly praying and thinking of godly things. Scripture states, "For our struggle is not against flesh and blood, but against the rulers, against the authorities, against the powers of this dark world and against the spiritual forces of evil in the heavenly realms (Eph 6:12, NIV)." These forces are in the second Heaven where the evil one resides and rules the air.

There are three parts to Heaven. The earthly atmosphere is where we reside and we see the clouds and birds fly this is called the first Heaven. (Genesis 2:19; 7:3, 23; Psalms 8:8, NIV) The area where the Sun, Moon, Stars, and other planets reside is the second Heaven known as outer space. (Deuteronomy 17:3; Jeremiah 8:2; Matthew 24:29, NIV) Then the area above the great "firmament" is where God and the Holy Angels reside and we do not have access to this Heaven in our mortal bodies. This is known as the third Heaven. (Deuteronomy 10:14; 1, Kings 8:27; Psalms 115:16; 148:4; 1Kings 8:27, NIV)

The mere voice of God is enough to make you sit up and take notice because it is a voice that you will not forget when He speaks to the masses. When God speaks to you individually, He uses a soft voice. The voice of God will not be mistaken for another voice. When God speaks He speaks with authority to convict your heart. "My sheep listen to my voice; I know them, and they follow me (Jhn 10:27, NIV)." The voice of Satan is a constant ring in your ear that will not go away. You will have to pray it away and still it will come back with a sneer of guilt if you yield to the voice. Your Spirit will question the prompting of Satan because it will leave you with many questions or uncertainty in your being. When you touch the hem of Jesus garments then you are changed from the inside out and you will know that the voice that is constantly rattling in your ear is not that of Jesus. Not that you will never sin again, but you will start to know the difference in the voices and begin to obey Jesus. You will know when you are sinning and you will start to correct your evil ways. Immediate repentance is eminent and then you can go on and do God's work but try not going back to your old ways. Not that you will not be tested, but work at it and ask God to help you so you will not commit the sin again.

The blood is found in the touch of the garment which is healing to the soul. One must experience the touch and voice of God speaking to your Soul and Spirit as you experience this miraculous conversion. You will begin to understand what God wants us to do on this earth. He wants us to save souls and keep his commandments and statues and most of all worship Him to the fullest. Remember to walk as God has commanded because He will carry your burdens for you to the cross of salvation.

# CHAPTER 4

## What Are God's Ways?

Gods' ways are not man's ways. God is our creator therefore, He thinks of Heavenly things and man thinks of earthly carnal things. The Bible states in Micah 4:2, NIV "Many nations will come and say, "Come, let us go up to the mountain of the Lord, to the temple of the God of Jacob. He will teach us his ways, so that we may walk in his paths. The law will go out from Zion, the word of the Lord from Jerusalem."

In Rev 15:3, NIV, "And they sang the song of God's servant Moses and of the Lamb: Great and marvelous are your deeds, Lord God Almighty. Just and true are your ways, King of the nations."

These words will be the words of the Saints that ascend to Heaven to be with the Father. The song will be one of joy and true happiness because they will be forever with God the Father, God the Son, and God Holy Spirit for eternity. God's ways are perfect, sure, right, and His statues and commandments are righteous and pure. (Ps 19:7-8, NKJV)

Obedience to the laws and statues God has set before is most important. But the first thing is to (as Jesus replied :)"Love the Lord your God with all your heart and with all your soul and with your entire mind Matt 22:37, NIV)." If you confess with your mouth that Jesus is Lord and follow the words of God then you will have ever lasting life with God who loves you more than you could ever imagine with our earthly minds. Every breath taken by you is breath from God who allows us to live on this beautiful planet.

Who is God? God is all knowing, loving, kind, patient, Omnipresence (God is present everywhere at the same time) and Omnipotent (having unlimited power; able to do anything), and Omniscient (all knowing). If you just take a moment and think about the three descriptions of God - you will be awed beyond reason because then you have been moved by your Spirit to be a real believer then you are ready to obey God.

Consequently the ways of God will no longer be a mystery. We as humans are so busy with the daily cares of this world, work, going to events, social media, eating, socializing, and finding the right partners for marriage that we don't let God into our daily routines.

The Hebrews had just crossed the Red Sea and saw the miracles of God and did not know where they were going or where their next meal would come from, however they reluctantly let Moses lead them in the wilderness but not without complaining and grumbling which is a sin. My point is they did learn to hear God and follow the law and statues. They let God step in and lead their daily lives. Just discern how other nations feared them and even today other countries want the land Jerusalem now occupies because it is blessed by God for His chosen people. There must be something wonderful about Israel for other nations to have wanted to obtain the land for centuries.  You might think the Jewish nation has some kind of power. Well, actually they do.  They have God (Adonai) who promised them that if they follow Him then they would inherit the land of "milk and honey" which is the land of Israel. According to Ezekiel 20:6, AMP "On that day I swore to them that I would bring them out of the land of Egypt into a land that I had searched out for them, a land flowing with milk and honey, the most glorious of all lands."

What most people fail to realize is the nation of Israel was originally made up of <u>many nations</u> and the ones who survived the 40 years in the desert became the "promised" people.  So they had to learn to believe, love, obey, trust, and worship the One and only God of the universe.  Once the Jews learned this valuable lesson then their lives were better but not without problems.  They prospered and God gave them what they needed for their daily living.

We can have the same thing once we get out of the way of our own flesh and let Jesus work with us through the Holy Spirit, then our lives will take on a whole new focus. God said "I will bless those who bless you, and whoever curses you I will curse; and all peoples on earth will be blessed through you (Gen 12:3, NIV)."  This is why the Jewish people have prospered through the centuries because of this blessing from God promised through Moses.  Nations around them will be blessed by God provided that they follow the commandments and statues set by Father God.  Our nations must continue to support and pray for the nation of Israel and the Jewish people everywhere, otherwise we will become the curse like nations that came before us.

One must understand these 10 Commandments and statues has always been in existence because these are the laws of Heaven that Satan broke. The pride in his heart which was a flaw in his character grew and festered in his heart because he wanted to be worshiped like a god which led to his destruction. Satan was the only angel God created besides man. Everything else was created through God "speaking" them into existence and then it came about.

God knew his perfect angel would fall and would consequently trick man and mankind would fall from grace. Satan did not know the all-knowing ALMIGHTY had plans already in place with His SON Jesus to redeem the world and take us to Heaven with HIM one day. You see once sin started God could not make the change. It was a contract that had to be completed to the end so that mankind and all angels would know that Adonai (God) is the Beginning and the End (Alpha and Omega) of all Creation. There are other mysteries that happened when Satan started his rampage on man that will not be revealed until the end of time, but know that God Almighty is in charge of everything and there are no "mistakes" in our lives or this life. You see God <u>wins</u> in the end so we don't have to worry because God has already <u>won</u> the race and Satan just does not know it.

God's ways are not our ways according to Isaiah 55:8-9, NIV "My ways are higher than your ways and my thoughts than your thoughts".

2 Cor 16:9, NIV "The Lord's eyes keep on roaming

throughout the earth, looking for those whose hearts completely belong to him, so he may strongly support them. But because you have acted foolishly in this, from now on you will have wars." God makes it very clear He is looking for obedience from man but because we don't have our hearts turned totally to Him then we will make war with each other and sin. If we don't obey then it is sin. Romans 14:23, NIV "But whoever has doubts is condemned if they eat, because their eating is not from faith; and everything that does not come from faith is sin." The scripture here says whoever has doubt is "condemned". This is a power packed verse because it says if you don't believe and have faith then you sin. So we must have faith in God otherwise we have sin in our life which is why we must pray and ask for forgiveness constantly since our flesh is bent on destruction.

## Gods' Heart

What is Gods heart? "I desire to do your will, my God; your law is within my heart." May the Lord direct your hearts to the love of God and to the endurance of the Messiah. (Psalm 40:8, NKJV)

2 Thessalonians 3:5, AMP" God's heart is the acknowledgment of our sins against Him and to obey His law and statues that is the basic requirement and to "Love the Lord your God with all your heart and with all your soul and with all your mind (Matt 22:37, NIV)." Once we fulfill this requirement then God can do His work in us. This is why Jesus came so He could "proclaim freedom for the captives and release from darkness for the prisoners" (Isaiah 61:1, NIV) set us free from bondage. This was Jesus's mission to be the approbation the Lamb who would take up our sins so there would be no more blood sacrifice done in the temple.

God really hated blood sacrifices because they really did not forgive sins forever just for that particular moment and the next moment someone would sin then an animal sacrifice would have to be performed. "What makes you think I want all your sacrifices?" says the Lord. "I am sick of your burnt offerings of rams and the fat of fattened cattle. I get no pleasure from the blood of bulls and lambs and goats (Isa 1:11, NIV)."

Our hearts should be atoned to Gods Word which is living everyday 24/7 of every hour of the day and looking to be righteous in the Triune's sight. We are destined to repent now or on the last day which is actually too late but every knee will bow to the SON of MAN. God does not want us to perish but to have "everlasting" life with Him in Heaven. We must humble ourselves before God and this is the only way to have God's heart and acknowledge the Creator of the universe. Many will disagree with this statement but scripture states "unless you change and become like little children, you will never get into the kingdom of Heaven (Matt 18:3, NIV)." We must be humble and have a pure heart like a child who has not been taught evil but will do as the parent tells them. One learns evil because our hearts are bent on this until the pure heart of God is given to us through godly parents praying for us until we know better, at the age of knowing when you become a teen at age 12. "Finally, brethren, whatsoever things are true, whatsoever things are honest, whatsoever things are just, whatsoever things are pure, whatsoever things are lovely, whatsoever things are of good report; if there be any virtue, and if there be any praise, think on these things. (Phil 4:8, KJV)."

"But a natural man does not accept the things of the Spirit of God, for they are foolishness to him; and he cannot understand them, because they are spiritually appraised (1 Cor 2:14, MSG)."

In Job 26:14, NKJV "Indeed these are the mere edges of HIS ways, and how small a whisper we hear of HIM! But the thunder of HIS power who can understand? He shall judge the world with righteousness and the peoples with HIS truth."

We are shown in the third part of the verse that God will judge the world with righteousness and his people will know His truth. What does the selection in the verse mean when it says, "He shall judge the world with righteousness?" God is perfect and no corruption is in Him therefore He does not have any corruption in the Heavens. He will refine Man of his corruption before he can come before the throne of God. This is accomplished by accepting Jesus Christ as your Savior and to acknowledge Jesus is the resurrected Son of God. This can be done by confessing your sins before God and asking Him to come into your life and you will make Him your Lord and Savior. Once you have asked for forgiveness then you can discover the righteousness God expects His children to have.

God will come and judge the ungodly after 1000 years of Satan in the depths of Hell. This will be the second death and will be the righteousness for the evil of mankind. Those who did not confess to God before the great and awesome day of The Lord will die a hellish death for ever in eternity in the flames of Hell. This is why we must be very prayerful and studying the Word of God always so we can keep our hearts clear and clean. We must hear the Word of God as we meditate on scriptures and not just read them but absorb the meaning of each verse until it becomes a part of you. Don't forget the scripture where the Rich Man asked Lazarus to dip the tip of his finger in *water* and cool his tongue, because he was burning in Hell. (Luke 16:24, NKJV) Remember Hell is very real.

The scripture says "Man shall not live on bread alone, but on every Word that comes from the mouth of God (Matt

4:4, NIV)." The Word is the Triune God (God the Father, God the Son, God the Holy Spirit) and God Almighty is the only one who makes it possible so we can get up every day to do the tasks before us. People just don't understand we are here by God's design therefore; we are to serve Him and Him alone. It has been stated over and over in the scriptures to the Jews and in the Hebrew Scriptures (Old Testament and Torah) that they would obey for a season then they would fall away back to worshiping the idols. Idols can be anything that is not of God such as; ungodly TV shows, obsessing over your technology gadgets, becoming a social media junky, your work, finding a mate, entertainment, buying merchandise, apps for profit and entertainment, things that have no real meaning in Heaven such as; money, cars, prestige in anything, recognition in the world, and power. Power is what got Satan in trouble and thrown out of Heaven. So it is with man, we want the same things that Satan offers under many different disguises. These disguises are not always easy to detect because Satan is so VERY crafty in his appeal to our fleshly selves. All we see is how we can get ahead and get the next deal done or how we can become so popular with our friends or career idol in the world. Who can we emulate in dress, sing, or act like a character in the movies rather than ourselves? Everyone wants power and to be recognized as a successful person. Even the criminal wants to be popular if that is to kill, steal then so be it. However, God wants truth and righteousness from us, so we have to be tried by fire in order to become true Christians. This means we will have many trials and tests to pass. God will know we are really for Him and not for the glory of ourselves. God is Holy and glorified not us.

## Simeon the Man Who Waited for the Birth of God

Simeon then prophesies "Behold, this child is set for the fall and rising again of many in Israel; and for a sign which shall be spoken against (Luke 2: 33, KJV)."

There are times when God allows us to see his majesty and awesomeness and this is when we should be alert and see what God has in store for us. Just as God promised Simeon he would not die until he had beheld the Son of God. Once he held God the Son in his arms the prophecy was fulfilled and Simeon knew the world would never be the same again. God gave Simeon a glimpse of His heart because God loved Simeon. Now this prophecy did not come true right-away but it took years but the promise was fulfilled. The radiant light coming from the small infant was a heavenly glow that Simeon saw radiating from the Holy Spirit of Jesus. This beautiful gift was to be shared with the entire human race and one day we would all bow down in the future to the most wonderful precious gift of love God could give humanity. Simeon touched Jesus and received the gift of love he had waited years to see before he was to die. The touch of the garment was the swaddling clothes of Jesus as a baby gave an old man hope of a new life for mankind on earth because he had seen the promised Messiah. "Master, now you are dismissing your servant in peace, according to your word; for my eyes have seen your salvation, which you have prepared in the presence of all peoples, a light for revelation to the Gentiles, and for glory to your people Israel (Luke 2:28–32, NIV)."

I remember a painting of Simeon and Jesus on the cover of the "Upper Room" daily devotional magazine. It was just beautiful to see a tear come down the face of Simeon as he was looking at the baby; it was just breath-taking. What made the painting more than just a painting there was a message imprinted in the artist vision? The artist painted the world inside the image of Simeon letting all who would look at the painting discovers the message of the cross. He would bring salvation to this evil world and everyone in the world would be saved. Jesus Christ was born to save all no matter what religious denomination or ethnicity they might be. All can be saved and come to God once the realization that there is only one God and He is *Adonai Jehovah* (the Lord our Master).

# Who Was Anna?

This poor woman also prophesied the coming King of Kings just as Simeon was praying.

In Luke 2: 36-38, MSG "Anna the prophetess was also there, a daughter of Phanuel from the tribe of Asher. She was by now a very old woman. She had been married seven years and a widow for eighty-four. She never left the Temple area, worshiping night and day with her fasting's and prayers. At the very time Simeon was praying, she showed up, broke into an anthem of praise to God, and talked about the child to all who were waiting expectantly for the freeing of Jerusalem."

This outpouring of the Holy Spirit in Anna and Simeon was an everlasting testament to God's love. Not only did she speak but was singing an anthem of praise to God for allowing her to also be a witness to the birth of the Messiah the promised King.

Both Simeon and Anna waited patiently for God to reveal something so big the Holy Spirit had to announce this monumental moment though a stirring in their Spirits. That something incredible was about to happen and they would announce the coming. Yet the announcement was hidden until the exact time when Mary and Joseph would appear at the temple for the celebration of Jesus circumcision (Bris in Hebrew). They would never be the same in their Spirits. Because knowing this child was like no other and He came to set the captives free from sin. His mission on earth would be eternal life and not of this world. The events that would take place because of Jesus coming would never happen again on earth is more than their Souls and Spirits could comprehend. The joy they felt was extraordinary peaceful and loving. They were given a glimpse into the Heavenly realm from the Holy Spirit which brought about an outpouring of overwhelming joyful songs and praise to God Almighty.

The parents of Jesus would be the gate keepers to keep Jesus safe and secure. Yet they had the divine privilege to raise not only God in the flesh but to be led by the promptings of the Holy Spirit to raise the child as God saw fit to have HIS SON raised by mortal man. How wonderful this is when you think about it. *Just the mere edge* of God the Father as to who HE really is and how everything is in such divine order lets you know who is in control of the universe. Nothing in this world just happens, but things happen because the Creator has command over our world. We are so accustomed to things moving in the flesh we really never take the time to see God is Spirit.

# CHAPTER 5

## Thunder of His Power

In Job 26:14, NKJV, reminds us who Almighty God really is"But the thunder of HIS power who can understand God? The Lord God's voice is like a roaring lion in the "Day of The Lord (Isa. 31:4-5, Jer. 25:29-36, NIV)."

The Almighty God will not spare anyone who is not of HIS kingdom and has not confessed their love for God and giving their heart to Jesus Christ.

In Jeremiah 25:25, NIV states that "The Lord will roar from on high; he will thunder from his Holy dwelling and roar mightily against his land. He will shout like those who tread the grapes, shout against all who live on the earth."

This prophecy statement is for the End Time that will come after the "catching up" of the Saints from the earth. God's voice is soft and pleasing but there will be a time in the End of Times where the wrath of God will come and HE will be heard and seen through-out the universe.

The Hebrews wanted to worship God at Mt. Horeb and wanted to hear God rather than Moses. So God stepped down to speak and the children ran because the Majesty of God's voice was more than they could stand with their unbelieving hearts and ears. (Ex 20:18-19, NIV) "When the people saw the thunder and lightning and heard the trumpet and saw the mountain in smoke, they trembled with fear. They stayed at a distance and said to Moses, "Speak to us yourself and we will listen. But do not have God speak to us or we will die."

The trumpet sounded (Gods' Voice) like nothing we can imagine or even think to hear coming from the mountain along with the fire the people were deeply afraid and ran with fear and asked Moses to speak to them and not God. For they were afraid death would come to them. Why would they think death would come? Because their hearts were still not right with God. Many of those *original* Hebrews were from many nationalities and countries. They came to know God when the plagues came upon Egypt. Therefore when it came time to migrate away from evil Pharaoh they were asked by Moses all who wanted to come with them come. They took on the title of Hebrew once they left the land of Egypt. These were the ones who lived among the Hebrews and had already known the customs but they were idol worshipers.

Moses led the Hebrews to the Mt. Sinai because this was the mountain of God where His temporary sanctuary resided on earth. God wanted the Hebrews to learn and to understand their rightful place with God. He wanted them to know and obey the commandments and statues that had been in place before the creation of the world.

The earth is full of His glory and the earth gives the radiance to God every day from the flowering trees, birds, beasts, sun, and moon in the galaxy and everything that lives on the earth or has breath. If we just take time and look at the earth for what it really is you will totally be amazed and awed by God's magnificent greatness and power. The Hebrew children could not understand that obedience was the key to know who God was at that time. But, they learned as many died from disobedience. The Hebrews had to live in the wilderness for 40 years until a time came when the grand-children would see the Promised Land.

Why is the voice of God so magnanimous? Because HE is I AM THAT I AM (Jehovah, YAHUWAH) and there is nothing more to be said. The Creator is awesome and powerful. HE is Adonai and HE will always be and has always been.

Man has not learned this great mystery. Even today with all of the signs pointing to the coming of Jesus the Messiah. Mankind is still resistant to believe in Jesus the Son of God. Many people have never heard of Jesus or what He did for mankind. The Millennial generation is really in the dark because they are consumed with what they can achieve now and have no interest in becoming Saints for Christ or knowing about God. Just ask the average 20 – 40 year old person and you will be truly surprised by the answers they give regarding; is there a God or where they will end up once they die. There is hope because God will release a powerful fire of the Holy Spirit on the earth and many young people will come to Christ during this End Time era. "In the last days, God says, I will pour out my Spirit on all people. Your sons and daughters will prophesy, your young men will see visions, your old men will dream dreams (Acts 2:17, NIV)."

Almighty God is so awesome it is hard to really describe HIM. God amazed Elijah and loved David the King. Yet David feared the wrath of God to the point he only wanted to please God. We have yet to really see the power of God on this earth. But as the End Times are unraveling we will see God's power and awesomeness. Mankind will be afraid and will come to Christ and know the Son of God. Many will perish because they cannot believe and will not believe because the sin and evil in their hearts. Therefore they will fall into damnation.

The Voice of God in the Holy Spirit is soft yet firm if you are really listening. The Holy Spirit will convict you when you are going in the wrong direction and not in the direction of obedience. Ezekiel described the voice of God and he said it was like "many waters" roaring when he saw the Lord sitting on his throne in Heaven. Ezek 1:24, NIV stated "I heard the sound of their wings like the noise of great waters, like the voice of the Almighty, the sound of tumult lie the noise of the host." The wings of the angelic beings that grace the throne of God have many wings and when they moved their wings sounded like God speaking. This is such a mystery because you cannot imagine with our minds the unique beings that surround the throne of God Almighty and how they are really intertwined around the throne of God. The outskirt of God's being is so enormous it cannot be numbered. The mere edges of God and his love for man and this world is just beyond what any mind can conceive and imagine.

No wonder the Hebrew children were afraid of the

voice of God. Since Ezekiel described the voice like many waters, the sound was very LOUD and ear piercing and the people were afraid. Moses was not afraid because he had been with God on the mountain for 40 days and had learned to hear the voice with his Spirit. He listened to the voice of God speak to him. He did not hear the same sound that the Hebrew people heard.

God is so full of love until it fills you with utter joy and warmth. "God said, "I will never leave you or forsake you (Deu 31:6 NIV)." Christians really don't want to stay on earth with all of the ugly evil things we have to contend with on a daily basis. This love God has for us is loving, peaceful, warm and like the best warm hug one could ever have and you don't want to let go. Because for the first time in your life you know you are truly loved as you were meant to be when God created the world for man. The ultimate test is to be obedient and follow the commandments God set for us and your life will be better but not trouble free on earth until the King of Kings and The Lord of Lords returns.

God gave His law and Commandments for us to learn and to keep them in our lives every day. We must eradicate our selfish thoughts that the devil plants in our minds daily, which keep us so busy that we cannot think to do as God wants us to do but what the enemy suggests. The devils deliberations are subtle but are constantly emitting all kinds of notions that are not godly and not relating to things Jesus Christ our Savior would have us do. Our Christian duty is to spread the word of Jesus to all our family, friends, coworkers, and those we meet along the way in our travels to and from our destinations. We must not get so consumed with what we have to do and who we are to meet that the message of the Messiah is pushed so far back into our minds that He is forgotten. Our titles on the job should not be a deterrent to whether we spread the Word of God or not. Our fruit should be kindness, humility, love, joy, happiness, and un-selfness. We should be the same all the time not when we want to be godly. We are known by our fruit according to scripture (Matt 7:16, NIV). We finally remember God when we go to bed or when we are finally sitting quiet and then we hear the "small voice of the Holy Spirit" speak to us. Then the "small voice" asks "did you spread my word today"? Did you study my word? Then we feel guilty because the devil comes quickly to say, we were disobedient. The real truth is - we allowed this to happen because we had the time, but we ignored the Holy Spirit speaking in our minds. We figured we could do the task later. Thereby later never came and on and on the cycle continues until we get into trouble. Then we want the Lord to help us, "he will not hear you" this is the devil's famous lie and we are condemned by our unfaithfulness. We proclaim Jesus will never hear us because we have not prayed or never prayed at all, now we feel unworthy to pray. This is another lie from the devil and all the more reason you should pray the prayer of forgiveness and ask Jesus to help you. Set aside time daily to worship, read, study, and listen to the Savior so that we can be the Christians we were made to be. When Christians obey God then they are not condemned, because they did as Jesus Christ asked according to scripture. The wonderful character of Jesus Christ is that He came to save us from our sins. He loves us so much He will love and forgive us up to the moment before we die. Just as the thief on the cross proclaimed his sinful life but recognized Jesus was the Son of God. Jesus had no sin and came to save us and the thief wanted to be with Jesus (Luke 23:32-43, NIV). Not only did he want eternal life but rebuked the other thief for saying blasphemous things to Jesus as he too was dying and going to Hell on the cross. He had a moment to ask for forgiveness of his sins and chose not to. There are always two sides to be considered on this earth. This is why God gave us "free will" to choose right from wrong or the "correct path or the wrong path". You choose Satan or God the darkness or the light. The love of Jesus Christ is so wonderful and awesome that it is so hard to describe that one can only moan within your spirit. When you truly come to know Jesus and who He really is, no earthly words can describe the feelings of love, peace, and thankfulness given by the Father.

We are given a choice every day to choose what we will do and who we will obey. Good or evil are the choices. We are bombarded with the cares of this world, TV, family, friends, Facebook, Instagram, tweets, all kinds of social media, games on mobile devices, job, money, relationships, and survival to get ahead or just exist with no hope. Those of us who choose to listen to the Holy Spirit and have a real relationship with Jesus Christ will move ahead and have a God-filled life which is prosperous in ways most people don't understand. People wonder why you are so successful in your life. Because you acknowledge your Heavenly Father daily and reject the naysayers. Naysayers are constantly making fun of you when you turn your back. They thrive on doing cruel jokes speaking profane talk and they think you are some kind of fanatic. Be zealous when you are being ridiculed by evil doers.  Just smile and walk away or have a godly answer will baffle your assailant even if it makes them angrier.  Evil people don't understand how you can walk away from confrontation so easily.  This is when the Holy Spirit is talking to you letting you know it is time to pray and let Jesus fight this battle.  He is waiting for you to evoke the prayer so He can start the process of making things right.  Let God have the glory and not the devil who has wanted the glory from the beginning of time. Now this might look like a cowardly act but it is not.  The thief recognized the glory of Jesus because Jesus forgave the people who were crucifying HIM as HE hung on the cross.  We are crucified daily by our enemy and we allow it to fester rather than praying and praising God for the many blessings He has already bestowed upon us.  Ask Jesus Christ to fight our battles and He will and you will be amazed how people will change their attitude and say things that only you will understand.  The naysayers will all of a sudden be kinder and even ask forgiveness to you and then you will know that only God could have allowed the Holy Spirit to do the work. Declaring the; HELP ME! Please Jesus! This small command gives Jesus the authority to do His best work to save you from more hurt but put a blessing upon you.  The other choice was to fight your enemy with curse words and retaliation of some kind which only ends up hurting you.   You cannot take revenge.  That is left for God to do.  You cannot rectify your situation with your human intellect.  Those who don't know Christ will only do what they know to do and that is to curse and swear and get vindictive because they don't know God. But this is where you come in to save folks who don't know God and help them to understand their life does not have to be hellish.  There is One who made them in His likeness who loves them and only wants them to choose the life of eternity and let Him lead their life. Many people will reject this notion to come to Jesus. Some will even know there is a God but the Spirit within them will not hear the call. God has to call them when they are ready to receive the Christian life after they have been beaten to the ground in the mud and mire of life this is when they can look up and say "God HELP ME". Once they are ready then Jesus will be able to help them. Again many will tell you, I don't want to know about God and leave me alone. This is where you walk away and pray for the person and let God handle this poor soul who will either continue to reject God and end up in Hell or finally come to reconcile their life to Christ and live with Christ in heaven as the thief did on the cross.

Jesus came to save the world and to set the captives free from bondage. (Luke 4:18, NKJV) "The Spirit of the Lord is with me. He has anointed me to tell the Good News to the poor. He has sent me to announce forgiveness to the prisoners of sin and the restoring of sight to the blind, to forgive those who have been shattered by sin." In this torn broken ugly world many are shattered by sin. People daily refuse to acknowledge Jesus and therefore they are living a life of brokenness. Many of today's Christians are "fence" Christians (those living on the fence of safety not HOT or NOT COLD but Luke warm) don't want to disrupt their lives of sin because it is too hard to do what God wants them to do. Therefore they continue with guilt every day and condemnation from the devil. The Holy Spirit speaks and says to them "don't do this or don't do that" you know that is wrong. But many are so hell bend on doing their own selfish ways of doing things until they cannot hear or know who God is. They clean up on Sunday to go to church and praise God but before they can leave the building they are already back into the same groove of disobedience. Many don't want to lose their friends and family members or better yet the social status that comes with being ungodly in this world. You become a leper if you truly worship God. Many Christians know this from experience. You will have very few friends and most will call you a religious fanatic, but I would rather be a religious fanatic than a hellish devil on this earth and end up losing my place in heaven and end up in Hell. You can lose your place and your name can be blotted out of the lamb's book. According to scripture you really have to believe in Jesus Christ as your Savior when you pray the sinner's prayer and really believe Jesus has saved you and not turn your back on HIM. If you turn your back on Jesus and continue your wicked ways as before with no remorse then you were not really saved. At this point it is really between you and Jesus Christ and no one else. Jesus makes the determination for your eternal destination since you did not resist the lies of the devil and repents of your sins then you will be forever lost. "All who are victorious will be clothed in white. I will never erase their names from the Book of Life, but I will announce before my Father and his angels that they are mine. "In Revelation 3:5, NIV verifies the above scripture and signifies this can happen. Moses knew it was possible when he prayed the following in Exodus 32:31-32, NIV "Oh, this people have sinned a great sin, and have made them Gods of gold. Yet now, if thou wilt forgive their sin - ; and if not, blot me, I pray thee, out of thy book which thou hast written." God's answer is found in verse 33: "And the Lord said unto Moses, Whosoever hath sinned against me, him will I blot out of my book."

In Psalm 69:27-29, NIV "Charge them with one crime after another. Do not let them share in your salvation. May they be blotted out of the book of life and not be listed with the righteous. I am in pain and distress; may your salvation, O God protect me."

Clearly in Psalm 69:27-29, it was made clear that your name can be blotted out of the Book of Life. Moses and Disciple John knew that your name could be blotted out of the Book of Life. But both knew it was a choice by the individual as to how and when he would ask for repentance or no repentance. In the book of John scripture says "My sheep listen to my voice; I know them, and they shall never perish; no one can snatch them out of my hand (John 10:27-28, NIV). " Because true Christians will obey and ask for forgiveness and Jesus has been given authority from God HIS FATHER to keep HIS sheep safe from the devil. But those who were perpetrating will be thrown into the lake of fire.

Scripture states in Rev 3:16, NIV "So, because you are lukewarm - neither hot nor cold, I am about to spit you out of my mouth" this is so awful for those who lived their life without wisdom and understanding but with contempt of God. Many people have different views on this subject but scripture is very clear at what it says and there is no interpretation; because scripture also says not to add to the word. In Rev 22:19 (NIV) "And if anyone takes words away from this scroll of prophecy, God will take away from that person any share in the tree of life and in the Holy City, which are described in this scroll." It also says in Prov 30:6, NIV "Don't add to his words, or he will rebuke you, and prove you a liar." The word is very clear and God's word never fails and is always true.

# CHAPTER 6

## "Just the Mere Edge of God", Job 26:14

What is this verse really saying to those who are Christians and those who are not a Christian? If you want true healing in your soul you will have to touch God, be a believer in Jesus Christ and believe that the Messiah came to save us from our sins. You must know He will come back one day and take us home to our real home in Heaven. You must believe in the touch of the garment of Jesus is just the healing that the nations and man needs to make his soul complete with joy, kindness, love, and happiness. God really intended that we would enjoy life with Him not with the things; we think we can get in this world. It is about God not us, but we have been brain-washed by the devil to think we don't need God and we need the things of this world to make us truly happy. When we actually figure out that the things of this world will not be enough to make us happy or fulfill the longing in our hearts it is almost too late to give our best to the Lord. Thank God for grace and mercy. God is so merciful and loving, He allows us to come to Him even with our last breath. We want to give God our very best and our very best years not a few years or a few seconds before we die. We want the crowns and the rewards Jesus has so promised that we would have if we give our lives to the Master. My point is our lives can be filled with a love that only God can give when we finally acknowledge and give our entire life over to Jesus, by doing this we are really starting to live the righteous life. Life will not be without troubles and heartache but to know God is there to comfort and protect you is the reward. When you pray you will receive peace that passes all understanding in life. You can talk to the Triune God and know He will answer your prayer and petitions for help. Now the help is not coming at a "microwave" pace that the world would have us believe we must live in the Masters timing.

Father God knows everything from the beginning to the end and how everything will finish this factual. We have no idea how things will come out and we want to fix everything and get our friends and family's view on everything instead of going straight to Jesus Christ and receiving a divine answer to our problems. I know this concept may be difficult to conceive. I have experienced divine intervention daily as well as deception, however; you will learn to decipher truth from error. But the flesh is not willing and the Spirit in us wants us to be more like Christ but we fail as Paul the Apostle stated, in Matt 26:41 NKJV "Watch and pray, lest you enter into temptation. The spirit indeed is willing, but the flesh is weak." We all fight this every day this is why we must pray when we find ourselves tempted to do what is not right." If we just remember that in God's eyes we are children then we will know what to do. Just as we give instruction to our children to do something and they don't do it, then you know your child has disobeyed you, therefore your action against God is disobedience. When we disobey the Father after He asks us to do something now and we figure we can do it tomorrow then there is a consequence. We did not obey God and we figure we can do the bidding of God at a later time. If our children don't do what we ask then they are punished or spanked depending on the offense. The same thing happens to us when we don't obey God. It is our life that is curtailed from getting the blessings we were supposed to get. Suppose you were told by God to go and check out the house you had been praying for today and you delayed several days you will lose the opportunity to buy the home God had for you. You are not the only person looking at the house and God said go and see it now but you delayed. The same scenario will happen to a job prepared for you if you delay and not go to the interview. The possibility of a delay because you did not listen to the "still small voice" of God is probable. Now you blame God for not getting the job or house but who is to blame for this disappointment and depression? You can only blame yourself because you were not listening or decided to wait (listening to the flesh) and lost the blessing that was meant for you. It only takes a few minutes a day to sit and be quiet and listen to God. Scripture states "Be still, and know that I am God!" (Psalm 46:10, NIV). Find a quiet place in your home and spend at least 15 to 20 minutes with God and don't say you don't have time. We have time to post to social media then we have time for God. Be quiet and pray and let God know what is on your heart and while you are quiet He will answer your petition. Once you get your answer, thank God and do as He asks you to do and your life will start to be more stable. Ask the Father to bless you with His Grace and Mercy every day and to bless your life and pour his "Favor and Prosperity" on your life and not Prosperity of money but of healing (a contented state of being happy and healthy and prosperous) then the monies will come. What is the Grace? Grace is a noun that means "Christianity, the free and unmerited favour of God shown towards man" this is what you want in your life.

"Whatever may be my task, I work at it heartily, as [something done] for the Lord and not for men, knowing [with all certainty] that it is from the Lord [and not from men] that I will receive the inheritance which is my [real] reward. [The One Whom] I am actually serving [is] the Messiah (Colossians 3:23-24, Amp."

"The Heavens declare the glory of God" (Psalm 19 1-2, NKJV) this is the magnificence of the Holy God in heaven because the Heavens show his everlasting work in creation every day on earth, that we don't seem to understand or see. Every day creation is creating something new from the breath spoken by the Word of God. It goes forth because this is a 24/7 creation from God for us to enjoy. We don't have any idea how magnificent and glorious this wonderful gift from God really impacts our lives. We just get up and go about our selfish lives doing whatever we want and not giving God a second thought and grieving the Holy Spirit daily because we don't acknowledge the Holy Spirit as a Spirit person. God gives the knowledge of creation day by day and night by night. However, we only care to minimize this information and to theorize the WORD of God. So by the time it reaches us it has no meaning on paper or in the book of the Bible. We listen to garbage all day long from media through the air of Satan and never think that the Social Media, TV, cell phones, and Computers can be learning tools for God. Who made these wonderful technological inventions? God made these things in heaven first He just loaned us the knowledge to invent them here on earth. They are for the building up of His kingdom not of Satan's kingdom. Technology can reach so many people throughout the world but we choose to diminish the values of this technology and let Satan have the power in the second heaven (the airways where the satellites reside to send the message of God) to overshadow God's work by listening and watching un-godly shows on TV that are vexing and contaminating our Souls on earth.

Psalm 19: 3-4, NIV reminds us that "the Stars have no voice yet it goes out to the ends of the earth." God is always creating new stars daily that we cannot see even with the satellites gliding through the heavens. They are held up in the heavens by a magnificent tent whereby the Sun resides with our Moon. Our galaxy is always creating new stars. The galaxy is forever expanding beyond what we as humans could ever hope to imagine and see with our earthly eyes. Scientists believe they see everything in the universe. However, new planets, stars, and galaxies are created daily and the creation story goes on for eternity.

Psalm 19:5-6, NIV "Gives the Sun its glory that it is hot with fervent heat and it gives light to all of the earth and the entire galaxy and no one can escape the heat of the Sun." This also describes Jesus Christ because He is always present and He is fire that will come back one day as a blaze of fire for his children.

In Psalm 19: 7-8, NIV,"The law of the Lord is perfect, reviving the soul. The statutes of the Lord are trustworthy, making the wise the simple. The precepts of the Lord are right, giving joy to the heat."

The Law of God has always been perfect from the beginning of time until eternity which never ends and will not change. God can restore the whole person if the person wants to know God. This is why the scripture says "making wise the simple" because what is wise to man without God is simple. But when man knows God's heart then he learns truth and then man becomes wise through the renewing of the mind and indwelling of the Holy Spirit inside of man.

"The precepts of the Lord are right, rejoicing the heart; the commandment of the Lord is pure and bright, enlightening the eyes" (Psalm 19:8, AMP). God's law will open our eyes to everything on earth and in the scriptures. Therefore our eyes will be open when we pray and have communion with God through the Holy Spirit who is all Truth will show you the way to live and be successful in life. Then your heart will rejoice because you are now really a part of God the Father, God the Son, and God the Holy Spirit. You have to be truly pure in heart, mind and Spirit.

What does pure mean? The Greek word for pure is Katharós (a primitive word) – properly, "without admixture"; what is separated (purged), hence "clean" (pure). The definition: clean, pure, unstained, either literally or ceremonially or spiritually; guiltless, innocent, upright.[5]

Therefore you have to keep a heart that does what God wants us to do and not what you want to do with your

---

[5] Strong, James, the New Strong's Exhaustive Concordance of the Bible, Comfort Print Addition., Thomas Nelson Publisher

evil Spirit. Constantly perceiving, thinking of God, and putting action to your words and deeds and not of the flesh. But be aware of the Holy Spirit, who will guide you to do what God wants when you ask to be led by the Spirit of Truth, in all things in your life. Not just some things but in everything you literally do every day. This is what it means to pray without ceasing.

1 Thess 5:17, NKJV "pray without ceasing" this is what God wants from us. The 9th verse of Psalm 19 gives a different perspective as to what is clean and what you should fear. The meaning of clean is the righteousness of fire that is given by God from his mouth and Word. Thereby being clean is the state of being purified by God's fire. God is fire and He removes all of the stains upon us when we ask for forgiveness with a reverent heart. Without bargains and saying we will never do the act again but with true sincerity.

The touch of the garment of Jesus is really touching God the Father, God the Son, and God the Holy Spirit. Touching God is perfect and just and righteous and the love which flows from the Triune God is so awesome no man can really explain the feeling of love that is streaming from the throne of God. Unless you really want to feel the love then you ask the Holy Spirit to show you His love. He will allow you to feel the TRUE God of the universe in a way that cannot be explained in this dimension where we live, but only from the dimension where God resides. This is where incorruptible bodies live with the Father.

Jesus is the only way to the Father. Once the feeble mind of mankind recognizes this, then man is ready to enter into a true relationship with God the Father, God the Son, and God the Holy Spirit. It is important to note the Holy Spirit is the one that passes on the inner-most secrets of God to man and gives us the true meaning and understanding of God's word and character. Once we understand this statute of God then man can come before the throne of God in purity and cleansing of his heart. We can hear the word and then praise God above all the earthly things here on earth as it is Heaven.

Just to touch or be a part of the magnificence of God is awesome but to truly know you have entered into the "holy of holies" is another matter. When you enter into the "holy of holies" you change from deep within your Spirit not just in the body. You become another person totally and you do not want to sin but you want to do what is right before God. All you want to do is to satisfy God and be obedient to Him who made you.

# God Is So Amazing

The Lord is so amazing in the things He does for us every day. If people would only listen to God - then their lives would be better. God only wants the best for his children and He only asks that we obey, love and give our complete lives to HIM. Jesus came to set the captives free not to bind us; but, we still don't understand what this means in Luke 4:18, NLT, "The Spirit of the Lord is upon me, for he has anointed me to bring Good News to the poor. He has sent me to proclaim that captives will be released, that the blind will see, that the oppressed will be set free." Also in 2Kings 6:17, NKJV, "Then the Lord opened the eyes of the young man, and he saw and behold, the mountain was full of horses and chariots of fire all around Elisha". Elisha prayed that the servant would see an amazing God overcome his enemy and trust God. This story is so awesome, since our eyes are so blinded to what is in the other dimension where God lives that we are not able to see into the spirit realm. When we ask for protection from God, He sends His Angels to protect us right away, because God loves us so much. Protection might not be the way we as mankind would like to see but believe me you are protected if you truly believe. He readily deploys a mountain full of angels of fire so we know He is real. The scripture states " And behold the mountain was full of horses and chariots of fire all-around Elisha". This event happened because the Syrian army was going to attack Israel and Elisha stated "Do not fear, for those who are with us are more than those who are with them" meaning the Syrian army that surrounded them in 2

Kings 6:16, 17, NKJV they had no idea they were out-numbered. The lesson taught by God was to trust Him and not look at your problem but focus on Jesus the Messiah and look up when problems arise. Put your trust in Adonai and your trouble will not go away but, you will know how to handle your problems because you will be armed with the Word of God. You will know certain scriptures to quote or where to find answers in the Bible to assist you.

Isaiah 45:7, "I form the light, and create darkness: I make peace, and create evil: I the Lord do all these things." (The Torah)

How amazing is our God. Adonai explained His awesomeness with this scripture because He said He makes all things and there is no other who can or will ever do or be the Master Creator. You really have to take an "AHAH" moment and sit down and really think about what was said by God in this scripture.

The Torah has a different interpretation that is more thought provoking than the bible interpretation. It is very clear God is in control of everything whether we think so or not but the Word of God is very clear. God creates light, darkness, peace, and evil and the evil is not related to what we have learned about God. But remember there was evil in the Garden of Eden. Satan was there who is evil and has been putting thoughts in our minds since the fall of Mankind. This is why God knew we would fall because Satan had already started his decent to fall from heaven when he tempted Eve and then Man fell from grace and was put out of the Garden of Eden by God.

God is love and he gave his creation free will. With our free will we can decide to love or not to love and this cannot be demanded by the Father but it is a choice to love God or not love God. When man ate the fruit on the tree of life then disobedience came into play and mankind made a willful decision to not love God and to love something else. Man chooses evil and not to be with God in the garden that was made for him. This willful act of disobedience sets the stage which was now on critical life support played right into God's plan to save His creation from sin and in the end mankind would be delivered from his disobedience. Mankind will now truly love God and will one day live with Him in Heaven after the Second Coming of the Messiah. "And be constantly renewed in the spirit of your mind [having a fresh mental and spiritual attitude], and put on the new nature (the regenerate self) (Eph 4:23-24, AMP)."

## "He Shall Judge the World with Righteousness and the Peoples with His Truth"

The Old Testament is comprised of the rules and regulations that mankind must follow to lead a Christian life. All of the rules and commandments that Moses gave to the Israelites were the foundation of Christianity. The Old Testament is comprised of history and prophecy for events that will come before the end. Since the Old and New Testament are merged together in a cyclical cycle then everything makes sense in creation, whereby the universe is a spiral circle. What once was will be again. Since Jesus the Messiah came over 2000 years ago then the Bible proves that He will come again to rectify the world and cleanse it from all un-righteousness. This is wisdom that has been spoken in the scriptures and through the Holy Spirit to many holy people through-out the ages. In order to become a true child of God one must allow the scriptures and the Holy Spirit to saturate your inner Spirit and Soul. Without this saturation and coming into the knowledge of God the Father, God the Son, and God the Holy Spirit then you cannot enter into the Kingdom of Heaven. The scripture states clearly that "to the one who is victorious and does my will to the end, I will give authority over the nations (Rev 2:26, NIV)." There is a record for everyone on this earth and everyone will have to go before the throne of God and give account of your life. Those who failed to get-off the fence will have to give an account of why they did not get rewards or a "crown of life" because they failed to full-fill the calling on their life. John the Disciple gives an account of what he saw in a vision of the Judgement for the lost and unrepentant souls; "And I saw the dead, the great and the small, standing before the throne, and books were opened; and another book was opened, which is the Book of Life; and the dead were judged from the things which were written in the books, according to their deeds (Rev 20:12, NIV)." Be a doer for Jesus because He gave so much for us and we can never reimburse, but we can give our lives to Him and believe in Him and we will see His true glory in Heaven.

All Praise and Honor given to; God the Father, God the Son, and God the Holy Spirit who will come very soon and take all Believers home to Heaven to be with them forever. Stay awake and alert and you will find the ". . . mere edges of His ways (Job 26:14, NKJV)."

Yerushalim Shalom Shaalu
"Pray for the peace of Jerusalem!" (Ps 122:6a, AMP)

# Appendix
## Names of God and Hebrew Words Used in the Book

**Adonai** – Hebrew name for God. Both "ADONAI" and "Elohim" Are Plural Hebrew Nouns "ADONAI"

**Almighty God** – (Having absolute power over all; Almighty) God having absolute power over all.

**Elohim HaAv** – God the Father

**Holy Ghost** - Ruach HaKodesh in Hebrew

**Jehovah** – JEHOVAH Ezer, the Lord our Helper

**Jesus** – "Jeshua" in English Bibles; Ezra 2:2; Neh 7:7). Yeshua, in turn, was a shortened form of the name Yehoshua ("Joshua" in English Bibles). Which means "*Yahweh* saves" (or "*Yahweh* is salvation").

**Jesus Christ** – Means; "Jesus Christ" is properly "Jesus *the Christ*." The one who saves.

**Jesus the Messiah** – Jesus the Anointed One

**Messiah** – Anointed One

**O Elohim** – Oh, God in Hebrew

**Selah** – Now, think about that!

**Triune GOD** - consisting of three in one (used especially with reference to the Trinity). The Triune Godhead. God the Father, God the Son, God the Holy Spirit.

**YAHUWAH** - I AM THAT I AM YHWH – God's unspoken name. God's Four-Letter Name: Yod-He-Vav-He or YHVH.

**Yeshua HaMashiach** - Jesus, the Messiah

# Bibliography

*The Amplified Bible, by* Zondervan Publishing House, *Copyright©* 1954, 1987, by Zondervan Corporation and Lockman Foundation., La Habra, CA

*The Holy Bible, New International Version,* Zondervan Corporation, Zondervan NIV Study Bible (Fully Revised Copyright ©1985, 1995, 2002 by the Zondervan Corporation, Grand Rapids Michigan

*King James Version/ The Amplified Bible Parallel Edition,* published by Zondervan *copyright©* 1954, 1958, 1962, 1964, 1965, 1987 by the Lockman Foundation, Grand Rapids Michigan

*New American Standard Bible,* published by Zondervan Copyright © 1960 - 1995 by the Lockman Foundation, Grand Rapids Michigan

*The Holy Bible, New Living Translation,* Second Edition, by Tyndale House Publisher, Inc. Tyndale House Publishers, Inc. copyright ©1996, 2004, 2007, Carol Stream, Illinois 60188.

Peterson, Eugene H., *The Message, The Bible in Contemporary Language,* NavPress Publishing Group, Colorado Springs, CO, The Message Numbered Edition copyright©2005.

Stanley, Charles F., the *Charles F. Stanley Life Principles Bible, the New King James Version,* Thomas Nelson, Inc. Copyright©2005 by Charles F. Stanley Nashville, TN

Strong, James, the *New Strong's Exhaustive Concordance of the Bible, Comfort Print Addition.,* Thomas Nelson Publisher, copyright©1995 Thomas Nelson Publisher, Nashville, TN

# References

Barras, Colin. (2013, July, 14) Volcano's screams may explain eruption's awesome power. Retrieved from News Scientist website: http://www.newscientist.com/article/dn23862-volcanos-screams-may-explain-eruptions-awesome-power.html#.VVNQdpOQwgQ, (accessed July 15, 2014)

Chadbad.org, on-line *The Complete Jewish Bible, The Torah* (Jewish Bible), © 1993-2014 Chabad-Lubavitch Media Center, http://www.chabad.org/,(accessed December 2014)

Josephus, Flavius, <u>The Works of Josephus</u>, translated by William Whiston, Hendrickson Publisher Marketing, LLC, ©copyright 1987, Peabody, MA p. 29-180, (November 2014)

<u>Merriam-Webster's Collegiate Dictionary</u>, 10th Edition, Merriam-Webster©Merriam-Webster, Inc. p. 952, Springfield, MA

Schneider, Aviel. (2013, May, 30). The Rabbi, the Note and the Messiah article, retrieved from Israel Today News, website: http://www.israeltoday.co.il/NewsItem/tabid/178/nid/23877/Default.aspx,(accessed May 31, 2014)

*Shroud of Turin Exhibition*, 2014 Royal Oak Michigan, Copyright © 2014 the Shroud of Turin. Visit to First Church of Royal Oak, Royal Oak, MI.,http://shroudexpo.com

# About the Author

Ardith Arnelle`Price is a spirit-filled Christian. She has had a wonderful relationship with Jesus Christ from her child-hood to the present. She is fervently seeking to spread the Word of God to un-believers and luke-warm Christians who are seeking answers to the meaning of life. She grew up in a god-fearing household where she learned about Jesus and how to live righteously as a Christian. Her early training from her parents made her the person she is today. She has experienced Jesus working in her life first-hand through her careers as music professional, Information Technology Manager personal relationships, church organizations, her Sorority, and various civic and public organizations that she has been affiliated with throughout her life. She has used her musical abilities through voice, violin, and piano to praise God and bring joy to so many souls throughout the world.

She received a Bachelor of Music degree from Fisk University, a Music Education degree/Choral and Music Teaching Certification from Michigan State University, Masters of Music from the Chicago Conservatory of Music, and advanced Information Technology studies at Lawrence Technology University.

She and her husband live in Southeast Michigan where they are college professors at a local community college. They convey the Word of God through their ministry.

Made in the USA
Columbia, SC
17 March 2021